Minding Our Elders

Caregivers Share Their
Personal Stories

By
Carol Bradley Bursack

MINDING OUR ELDERS
CAREGIVERS SHARE THEIR PERSONAL STORIES

Author - Carol Bradley Bursack
Cover Design - Kyle Alcott
Publisher - McCleery & Sons Publishing

International Standard Book Number: 1-931916-41-1

Printed in the United States of America

To
Clarence Little Bradley
and
Ruth Elaine Sandin Bradley

Foreword

During a twenty year period, when my husband and I were taking care of our parents, I became an astute student of the caregiving process. Although I learned a great deal about the mechanics of caregiving by doing it, I still questioned my feelings of frustration, guilt, stress and burden, along with other feelings of pride and accomplishment for a job well done.

In an effort to understand the total caregiving process, I went back to school and wrote a dissertation on caregiving of elderly parents, which was based on interviews with the "experts in my midst." This whole experience helped me ferret out a few epiphanies (tiny moments of clarity) that gave me comfort, and helped me to see the purpose of going through this process; to develop the integrity and understanding I needed to enter the final stage of my own life-cycle.

Carol Bradley Bursack also turns to the caregiving heros in our midst, who have *been there - done that!* Carol relates caregiving experiences of her own and those of her peers in a delightful, well-written, and *"oh, so real"* book. Her stories give you a glimpse of what it's like to grow old, and how the caregiving process is carried out. Hopefully, during the laughing and crying, you will develop a few epiphanies of your own as you read this heartwarming book.

Mary Ellen Erickson, Ph.D.
Author of *Common Sense Caregiving*

Acknowledgements

I *had* to write this book. As my caregiving years piled up, my contacts with other caregivers grew, and their need to talk about their caregiving issues was clear. My own feelings were just as strong. I simply had to write.

When I wrote *Minding Our Elders: Caregivers Share Their Personal Stories*, three of my elders were still alive. They are all, now, at peace – their frail bodies dead, their spirits free. The time feels right to publish.

My gratitude first goes to my sons, Adam and Jason. Even though much of their childhood included watching me fly off to take care of some elder emergency, they have remained strong and supportive. Even though an elder care book is unlikely to be their choice of entertainment, they have always cheered me on. They've recognized my mission. Jason's wife, Diane, has been a joy, and her additional support is a blessing to me.

To my sister, Beth Bradley Walter, also a key caregiver to our parents, thank you. I would have gone nuts without you. To my brother, David Bradley and Dave's wife Joyce – you've lived too far away to give hands-on care, but you did a lot. Thank you for your ongoing support and cheers.

Thanks to the wonderful staff at Rosewood on Broadway; I want to name you all, but there is not room. Fifteen years is a long time, and that's how long I had at least one person in your facility. So, from the bottom of my heart, thank you for caring for those I've loved. You helped give me peace when I thought I couldn't do it anymore.

To Forum Communications Company, specifically The Forum – thank you. I'm deeply grateful to Mark Glaser for hiring me after I'd been out of the traditional job market for 20 years; to Andrea Hunter Halgrimson for hiring me in The Forum library; to The Forum's former Managing Editor Carole Tarrant for pushing to make my elder care column a reality; and to Dean Rhodes for placing my column in the best position possible. This column has given the issue the visibility it needs, and I couldn't have done this without The Forum and you special people.

Thank you to Gail Gabrielson for her editing skills and for her support. Thank you to my kindred spirits Sue Scott Campbell, Jane Lundberg and Karen Hanson, women who encouraged me during times when I was drowning in negativity.

And to the caregivers themselves, the people who shared their personal stories – there are no words to describe my gratitude. Without you, the book would simply be one family's memoir. Your stories make *Minding Our Elders* universal. I am deeply grateful for your willingness to talk about your very personal experiences.

Introduction

Fargo, North Dakota. Separated from Moorhead, Minnesota, by the silty, serpentine Red River, Fargo is my home. With the exception of a couple of years in Europe and a year in Colorado, I've lived my life on the great, grassy northern plains. It's here in Fargo that I wrote this very personal book.

I could, however, have spent my life living in Ohio, Texas, California or New York and written essentially the same book. The subject is universal. Baby boomers are now facing the challenge of caring for their aging parents, and that challenge knows no borders. Some version of what has happened to the elderly people in my life and in the lives of the people I've interviewed, is happening or will happen to you, the reader, as well.

Many of our elderly parents took their last breaths in a nursing home. Their health had deteriorated to a point where they couldn't safely stay in a family environment.

You'll read of the turmoil many of us went through as we settled our loved ones in Rosewood on Broadway, or Elim, or Eventide. Homes in other areas will have different names, different physical configurations, different staff. That's immaterial. You'll go through the same agonizing process as you look for the best quality care available. You'll go through the same confusion as you try to find a way to work your parents' new environment into your own life.

Some of our people are fortunate enough to die with family, in their own homes. Others die in a hospital. Some cling to a whisper of life in a nursing home. But for all, eventually, their journey must end. *Minding Our Elders* was written to support you as you travel the last leg of their journey with them. It was written to remind you that you are not alone.

Carol Bradley Bursack

Table of Contents

Chapter 1
Minding Our Elders: Prologue

A small breeze sifts through the screen, then sneaks around a cracked open window, carrying the rich scent of fall harvest from fields surrounding Fargo. Dad's horn-rimmed glasses sit on the tip of his nose, well below his foggy hazel eyes. There's a sore forming on his parchment cheek, evidence of a long ago summer spent digging fossils under searing prairie sun. His square jaw nearly pokes through his skin, while his gray-brown hair fuzzes up in tufts like a pile of down.

He smiles that deep, crinkly smile of my childhood, and gestures toward the books squeezed against his TV: law, debate, chemistry, physiology, philosophy. Toward the degrees and awards crowding the wall; much of it computer generated, made-by-loving-hands-at-home evidence of his delusional accomplishments. Toward the briefcases stuffed with letters written, forged and delivered by his personal representative of suspended reality – me.

"Thank you for helping an old man's fantasy," he says.

For a moment, my dad of old emerges from the confused layers of his damaged brain. He looks into my eyes and he understands. A couple of bricks fall from my shoulders, lightening my load.

"I'm glad I can help," I say next to his ear.

I put his razor in the drawer and set up his CD player with *The Best Of Benny Goodman*. His lower dental plate glued, I check for feedback on his hearing aids. The batteries are okay.

"You look good today," I say. "See you tomorrow at lunch. Vaya con Dios." I pick up my coat and ratty, rose-strewn duffle, then blow him a kiss.

"Vaya con Dios," he says. Go with God. A remnant of his once fluent Spanish, now faded to a few lonely words that sweeten his disjointed speech.

I wind my way down the hall, through wheelchairs, med cart and walkers, nestled in a cocoon of creamy papered walls touched with teal and pink, oak furniture, nostalgic pictures and lace. The aroma of coffee sails above the vinegary odor of morning meds. A toaster pops in the kitchenette. Plates of bacon and scrambled eggs, dishes of oatmeal, and multiple side dishes of prunes are set on the tables in front of residents no longer interested in food.

As I walk toward my mother's room, I see faces that are as familiar to me as my friends'.

"Hello, Jesse! You look so pretty in your pink dress!" I say. Little Jesse, whose age and weight approximate one another, looks at me.

"Are you going down yet?" she asks. Jesse's afraid of taking the elevator alone.

"Not this time," I tell her, "but you can go with me when I do."

"Hi, Selma," I say. Selma, now in her seventies, has been a child all her life. She holds out her arms when she sees me go by.

"I need a huugg," she says.

"I need one too, Selma." I hug her and move on.

"Hi, Sarita," I say as I walk by the nurse who is coaxing Lloyd to eat some tasty medicinal mush. Sarita's smile charms him and he gums down the brown goo. "Is Alice still at breakfast?" I ask, knowing my mother-in-law usually eats in the dining room at this time.

"She went down quite awhile ago," she says, wiping Lloyd's chin.

"Morning, Sandy," I say as I walk by an aide hurrying toward a call light. "I see Dad needs his shampoo. I'll bring it tomorrow."

"Well, it's about time!" Sandy answers. "You never do a thing around here." She laughs her hearty, healing laugh, and shakes her head in mock disgust.

I reach my mother's room at the end of the hall. She looks fragile and small in her scaled-down recliner. Her silver hair still holds a bit of its natural curl – the curl I didn't get. Her burgundy embroidered sweatshirt with its little pink collar, blends with the pinks and blues of the room. She has a good start on the crossword puzzle in *The*

Forum.

"I couldn't believe how clear Dad was this morning," I tell her. "Underneath it all he really does know we're playing a game." Her eyes fill with tears.

"I think he does," she says.

"I brought a bunch of stuff today." I pull out a huge blue jar of skin cream, a tube of toothpaste, and three clean glasses – she likes glass, not plastic – so I take home her dirty ones and bring her clean ones each day.

"Oh, I brought some popcorn, in case that sounds good. They'll pop it in the microwave whenever you want it."

"I'll get you some hot coffee while I'm down getting your ice," I tell her as I unpack her cheese and crackers. After throwing some clothes in the laundry, I cross the hall to the stairway door, push the alarm release, open the door, do a quick bend and swoop from the waist, slip under the protective strap and go down to the first floor nutrition center.

Rushing icecubes clatter and crash from the machine into my plastic container. I pop a tiny sliver into my mouth, cover the bowl, take a cup from the rack and pour some coffee, then carry it all to the dining room to see if Alice is ready to go back to third floor.

Alice, my mother-in-law, sits at her table, clear white hair sparkly in a sea of dull grays and yellow-whites, her cornflower blue sweater buttoned high around her chin, yellow terrycloth bib rumpled in her lap. She's holding her spoon in mid-air, staring straight ahead at yesterday. As I walk up beside her, she startles, then laughs.

"You caught me," I say. "I was trying to sneak up on you! Are you done eating? Did you have enough?"

"Oh, I don't know." she says.

"It looks like you had a good breakfast," I say. "Why don't you come up with me? Your church *Messenger* came and I put it in your room. You'll want to look it over." Alice nods, and I help her up. She looks around as I aim her toward the elevator, then begins pushing her walker ahead.

"Hey! Hey, Bluey! Take me up with you!"

I glance down at my denim shirt and know that I am being

summoned. Victoria has been sitting guard by the lobby door; short, straight gray hair and scowling face set above her favorite red sweater. She's in her very personal spot with the side table pulled up the exact number of inches. Now she's decided it's time to go back to third floor and tell them what a horrible job they are doing in this place.

"Sure, Victoria, I'll take you up," I say. After putting the ice and coffee in a corner of the elevator, I unlock the brakes on Victoria's wheelchair and push her in. "Watch out for my feet!" she screams. "That big oaf, don't let him near me! Hey! Don't let him on!" She flails her arms indicating Frank with his cart and oxygen tank. "Don't touch my feet! My feet! Take me up and put me by the drinking fountain!"

I settle Victoria in the elevator and help Alice scoot herself on, placing her as far from Victoria as possible, just in case the queen starts swinging. Frank wisely decides to wait for the next round.

"Victoria, where are Sissy's pennies?" I ask. She looks at the doll in her lap and probes the little pockets of the checkered apron.

"Somebody stole 'em!" she growls. "I'm gonna sue!"

"Oh, I'll bet the pennies just fell out," I say.

"No, they didn't!"

"Here. I've got some pennies." I take two pennies out of my jeans pocket and slip one in each of Sissy's pockets. Victoria grabs my head and kisses me. I kiss her back. The elevator stops.

"We're here, Alice. Do you want your chair by the elevator or do you want to go down to your room?"

"About half way, I think," Alice says. I try to read her and decide that maybe her room would be best since she has some mail she can look at.

"Let's go down to your room," I say. "You get started and I'll catch up after I get Victoria off."

"Put me by the water fountain! No! Move me over more. A little farther! There, that's better." I leave Victoria in her spot, the exact distance from the water fountain she requires.

I retrieve the ice and coffee and catch up with Alice, who is standing in the middle of the hall gazing. "They stretch the hall longer every day, don't they?" I say. She laughs and starts walking once more. We inch our way down the hall until we get to her room. The last one on the left. Across the hall from Mom. Down the hall from Dad.

"Here, I'll turn on your light so you can read a bit," I say. I arrange her night stand, water her mum and coax her to sit down and rest her legs. She thinks awhile and finally sits. She smiles and looks toward her newsletter.

"Bye," I say. "I'll be here for lunch tomorrow. You've got chapel this afternoon. Someone will remind you." I wave, then pick up the ice and coffee. Across the hall at Mom's, I leave the coffee on her table, deposit the ice in her cooler, and pick up my jacket and tote.

"See you tomorrow," I say.

"What's a three letter word that means "way cool"? she asks.

"Huh?" I say. "I'll call you if I think of it. You call me if you decide to cheat or figure it out. See you at noon tomorrow."

Once more I move toward the stairs. I push the alarm release and try the knob. The alarm shrieks. My face burns as I punch in the code. Scrambled. In answer to the flashing lights and air-raid squall, three pair of feet thunder toward me. I punch the star button and re-enter the code. Silence.

"Soorrry," I call. I open the door, bend and swoop my way under the strap and down the steps, dodge residents as I make my way through the hall, and out the door. The sun is still high enough to share some warmth, and I let my jacket fly. Tomorrow, I'll visit at noon.

***

"Am I doing this right?" Steve asks when I talk with him about how caring for his mother is affecting his life.

"I do it because it's the right thing to do," Ann says when she tells me her story.

"He simply can't deal with it," Susan says of her brother.

"I had to think who needs help the worst? – my parents' or my kids," Julie says.

Caregivers have questions. They want to talk. They want to talk about how to do this life. One in four of us is taking some responsibility for the care of the older generation, and that number is growing as better medical care helps people live longer, often in poor mental or physical health. Unlike past generations, many boomers had their children at a later age, more women have outside jobs, families are separated by physical distance and multiple marriages. So sometimes we get frustrated. Or sad. Or just plain tired. Often we simply need an empathetic ear.

Minding Our Elders is our way of lending an ear to one another. It's been percolating for all the years that I've been caring for our family's older generation. During ten of those years I spread my time between my family members still in their own homes and those in Rosewood. I became well acquainted with firefighters, the emergency room, monitoring devices, home health services and clinic staff members. Evenings, I'd live in fear of the ring of the phone. The fear that the call was another emergency. It often was.

Then my mother, the last elderly member of my family at home, went into Rosewood. My time spent at Rosewood on Broadway was substantial enough that most of the residents and an occasional staff member thought I worked there. To find a bra that needed mending, half a hearing aid, or an upper plate with a chipped tooth in my pocket was simply normal. My daily tote to the home would include soda, wine, cheese, candy, magazines, mail, computer-generated awards and degrees, favorite toiletries.

As I've traveled this road, I've met other caregivers doing the same. We've visited on the snail-paced elevator at the nursing home. We've shared our stories while ducking the wind by the vestibule door. We've cried leaning against our cars in the parking lot. When we greet each other in the grocery store, we say, "How's it going?" We all know what *it* is. We've been torn between love and exhaustion, dedication and guilt. Most of all, we've wanted to do the right thing.

Listening to my friends' stories helped pump me up. I'm told my stories help them as well. So we're offering our naked, sometimes painful, stories to you, with the hope that you, too, may benefit. A few people have requested that I drape their stories in a towel of anonymity, and I've complied by changing some names and identifying characteristics. We think you'll understand.

Joseph Slaperud

Chapter 2
Fly Away, Joe

The squeal of Joe's hearing aid joined the twittering of hungry sparrows gathered for lunch. Joe teetered out on his wishbone legs to the edge of his one step, then tottered on down into his yard, one hand sliding along the clothesline behind his 1920's bungalow, past the plastic tube feeder, still half full of mixed seeds for the wild birds, past the wood feeder the blue jays had emptied, until he got to his garage door.

There he filled a grimy ice cream bucket with seed. He swayed with the wind as he brushed a white hair from his eye, then picked up the bucket and wobbled back toward the feeders, grabbing the clothesline once more for support. He filled the wood feeder with sunflower seeds. The jays also liked peanuts, so Joe reached around his stomach into his jeans pocket and pulled out some peanuts in the shell, then placed them in the feeder.

"There ya go," he said, his voice grating like a motor run dry. He put the bucket back in the garage. A zillion tweets and chirps followed him back along the clothesline, up one step and into his house. Now he would sit at his kitchen table, sipping vodka and orange juice, and watch until supper.

We'd been neighbors for years. We'd wave in passing and occasionally I'd help Joe and his wife Alice carry in groceries. They were both frail, but "got along," as folks say around here. Then Alice died. I intended to just pay my neighborly respects, but somehow I couldn't leave this deaf old man by himself. His need met my need, and we became a team. I visited daily.

We communicated with facial expressions and gestures, but most of all through notes. I wrote. Joe talked. Joe had been a young telephone engineer when he lost his hearing. He was scrappy and inventive and continued to work, with electronic help, until his retirement. He wore the old kind of hearing aid that plugged into his ear, with wires trailing down his chest to a battery pack in his shirt pocket. While the receptors in Joe's ear lay dormant, the world could hear the aid wail.

Each of my visits would leave pages and pages of half-conversations and nonsense strewn across his kitchen table, butter smeared from the popcorn we'd munch while we chatted. My young boys delighted Joe. They'd go with me to visit and watch his emerald-hued, captioned TV or play in his musty attic. They'd come for pizza and treats. I reinstated the tradition of setting up and decorating the old bottlebrush Christmas tree my boys found in his attic. I ushered him through cataract surgery and administered drops. We'd sort his mail and make his appointments.

Once every few weeks, my boys and I drove Joe to visit his older sister in Mayville, about an hour drive from Fargo. A few miles out of Fargo, Joe would squawk, "Jason, what's the next town?"

"Gardner," Jason would say.

Joe would look at me; I'd nod that Jason had answered. Joe would then reach into one of his bulging pockets, pull out a fistfull of golden butterscotch coins and red and white stripped mints. He'd toss some over his shoulder, and Jason and Adam would scramble around the back seat retrieving sweets. The trip was officially underway.

Joe marked miles with stories of attending first grade only speaking Norwegian and having to repeat the grade after learning English. He told of stacks of dried lutefisk leaned up outside store walls all winter to stay frozen. How dogs came by and relieved themselves against this delicacy. No matter. The lye-soaked codfish appeared on Christmas tables with great celebration, gloriously boiled and covered with butter. Quite a treat, he assured us. We learned about Prohibition. About hip flasks and moonshining.

One day I wrote, "Joe, let's get a bird!" I drove him to the pet shop at West Acres Mall and Joe chose a soft turquoise bit of fluff. We bought a cage, toys and food and brought the terrified little parakeet home in a box.

"I'm naming him Nuts." Joe said.

"Nuts? How come?" I wrote.

"Because he's nuts," Joe answered, shrugging in his "why not?" way.

Whether the bird liked the name or not, he loved Joe. They were devoted to each other. Joe sang to Nutsie daily, a yowling rendition of "Sweetheart of Sigma Chi," the only tune he could remember. I took Joe on two trips to New Jersey to see his family. I took him to dinners hosted by the Telephone Pioneers of America. I brought him food and tried to make sure his bills got paid.

One year I bought him a new address book and we attempted to fill it in. I wrote down a name from the old scratched-over pages and looked at him.

He responded. "Forget him, he's dead!"

"Oh," I said as I nodded.

I wrote the next name.

"He's dead, too," was the response.

"Her?"

"Dead."

"How about him?"

"Not sure."

"Tell you what, Joe," I wrote. "Let's do this another day." We never finished that project.

I would check Joe's movements at night by the glow of his lights and felt relief when I knew he had gone to bed. He'd had many falls, and I'd ridden in a few ambulances with him. He dislocated his shoulder, cut his head badly, messed up his face.

One evening, as I pushed a pork roast into the oven, the phone rang.

"Is Carol there?"

"This is she."

"Carol," the voice said, "Joe's alarm has just gone off. Could you go over and check on him?"

Joe had an alarm, a Lifeline, which hung from a chain around his neck and was set to ring a phone at an emergency station. He had pushed the button, which then alerted the attendant in the emergency room. He usually left the alarm on his bed stand, but would wear it if I put it on him during my noon visit, as I had earlier that day. They kept my number to call so I could check on him when it went off.

I ran out my door, across the yard, through his living room and into Joe's kitchen. He was spread out on the floor. I'd found him like this before, but this time was different. The angle of his leg was creepy.

"Help me get up," he croaked. I pulled a kitchen chair over to brace him, as I had done so often before. Normally, through pushing and pulling, I could get Joe up far enough so that he could help himself into the chair.

I shook my head, got some paper and wrote, "You're hurt, Joe. We'd better get help."

He protested, tried to move, lay back wincing. I called the attendant back and said to send the paramedics. We rode an ambulance to the hospital; Joe was admitted; he was operated on and placed in a room with three others. I still visited daily. But I never again saw him smile.

Rosewood had an opening just as Joe was discharged from the hospital. They graciously accepted Nutsie as well. I brought pictures and mail. His friends brought his television set. I told him that his son was coming to celebrate his birthday. Nothing excited him. Nutsie moped by Joe's bed.

I was eating supper with my family when the phone rang.

"Carol. This is Dorothy from Rosewood. I'm so sorry to tell you this, but Joe died. He was fine this afternoon. There was no warning."

I knew that. I'd seen him two hours earlier.

I went to Rosewood to see him one last time. His was the first raw dead body I had ever seen. No funeral home magic. An empty cage. I knelt by his bed and cried.

Nutsie and I drove home.

Chapter 3
Susan

Dried leaves from the parking lot blow with me through the double doors of Mexican Village. I close the first door, walk through the second and am welcomed by canned Mexican music and the fragrance of enchiladas. Hot oil snaps from a plate as the waitress walks by in the dining room; my mouth waters on cue. I check in and am shown to a reserved booth.

The room's starting to hum as business people hustle in for lunch. I see Susan and wave. Susan's a 43-year-old computer programmer with a dramatic sense of style. Today it's western. Her shoulder-skimming blonde hair dances with curl, large bronze horses hang from her lobes, her jean skirt swings freely around her western boots.

I glance down at my jeans with the bleach spot (it's just a small one), and my rumpled peach plaid flannel and realize I forgot to change clothes.

As Susan slides into the booth, the waitress arrives. They know each other and chat a bit, then we greedily receive our chips and sauce and order our chilies relleno. After a quick catch-up on kids and life, I ask a few pointed questions and Susan dives into her story.

***

Up until Dad died, Mother was just Mother. She had always depended on him, and he made most of the decisions, so any mental decline wasn't terribly obvious. Religion was Mother's territory, the rest belonged to Dad. That's how we grew up.

We were really a pretty dysfunctional family, I guess. The atmosphere was repressive. Dad wouldn't tolerate any rebellion and Mother's religion was so strict there was no room to breathe. A feeling of closeness just wasn't there.

I was bright and my dad appreciated that, but I was physically a late bloomer and couldn't please Mother with my looks. I was also very up front and sharp tongued. Mother was interested in appearances, physical and social, so this caused problems for us. With her, as long as everything appeared fine, it was fine.

I don't want to be misunderstood. I love my mother, and I'm glad I can help her at this time of her life. Even though she was often superficial, she could be a lot of fun. In fact that's one of the hardest parts of watching this deterioration. I've reached a time in my own life when I have more freedom and I would love to be able to travel with Mother and have fun. But now that's impossible. She can't be away from her things, or she gets disoriented and really kind of nuts. It's painful and frustrating for me to watch.

I was the middle of three girls, with Ron, my brother, being the oldest child. My parents doted on Ron. One of his favorite expressions when we were growing up was, "I can do no wrong!" And that seemed to be true. But after Dad died, when Mother's deterioration started to show, he really didn't want anything to do with the situation. Ron and my youngest sister Marg live in Minot where we grew up and where Mother still lives. But they stay pretty aloof from her problems. Marg teaches nursery school and has young kids, so she's busy.

And Ron...just keeps his distance. He simply can't deal with it.

Ann, my other sister, lives in Denver, and I live in Fargo. After Dad died and we were wondering how to handle Mother's situation, Ann had said Mother could live with her. I drove Mother to Denver so she could see what it was like. I really wanted Ann to observe her anyway, because I could see she was deteriorating mentally and Ann is in social work and sees a lot of older people.

What happened then was interesting. When Mother and I got to Ann's, I looked into a day care agency so Ann could drop her off while she was at work. Then I said I was leaving so they could see how it'd work out. Well, it didn't work at all. Ann meant well, but as soon as she had Mother alone a little bit she told me, "I can't do this. You've got to take her back. She's upset without her things and confused being away, and won't adjust to the day care. It's too much for her and for me."

I drove Mother back home and we eventually moved her into a very nice apartment in Minot. We arranged for several hours of home care from a local agency, but that didn't last. She wouldn't let them in, and if they did get in, she got abusive. She shoved and punched and pinched them so they refused to come back. I knew we needed to do something. It was scary and exhausting.

While we were working it all out, I brought her to Fargo for cataract surgery. What a nightmare that turned out to be! Looking back, it was poor planning on my part, because I had just had surgery myself and wasn't feeling too well yet, but Mother couldn't stay in her apartment alone and her eyes had to be done, so this seemed like the time.

I had Mother with me two months. The whole time was a battle. She couldn't remember not to scratch her eye after surgery. I'd say, "Mother, you can't touch it!"

She'd say, "But it itches."

We'd go round and round. Everyone would remind her. I had signs up all over the house. It did no good. She needed drops four times a day. She wondered each time what I was doing. She just couldn't get it. I would be patient at first, but about the sixth time I explained the same thing, I would get snippy.

I try to work on my sharp tongue, but it is an integral part of who I am. I have always been open and honest. I don't - can't - hide my feelings. Maybe it isn't all bad, because Mother would say, "At least I know where Susan stands." That may have been a positive thing in her confusion. But I do have a lot of guilt.

I started handling Mother's finances right after Dad died. She had no ability to finish a task, so I took it over. Ann was too far away, Marg didn't have the time and Ron just wasn't interested. I didn't mind, except now Mother kept accusing me of making her move in with us and of wanting her money. I would say, "Mother, you are just visiting, remember? You had eye surgery and you're getting well."

She would go on snooping binges, digging through all of our stuff until she found something that interested her. When she would run into her own records, she would hide things.

I can get really angry with her, but when I do she seems to get it. I don't like it when I get angry, because I know she can't help her confusion, but it seems to be the only thing that works.

After two months, I'd had it. It was March and we were in for a fierce spring storm, but I didn't care. Mother was down to one eye drop each day, and I felt it was time for my sister to help. I called Marg and arranged for her to meet us part way, in Jamestown. I told Mother, "You're well enough to go back to Minot, now, so Marg is driving to meet us in Jamestown. You'll go back with her." I kept talking about the drive to Jamestown, and soon we were on our way.

My husband Al came with us. I was driving, and not a bit happy. The roads were snow packed and slippery and the visibility was horrible. The wind had to be forty miles an hour and the snow was swirling and drifting. Mother was dead silent. I sort of noticed, but was too busy driving to care. After awhile, I said to Al, "I can't do this anymore. You need to take over."

We switched places and then I became more aware of Mother's silence. Suddenly she screamed, "I'm not crazy and I'm not going to Jamestown!"

"Oh, God," I thought, "poor Mother!" Jamestown is where the State Mental Hospital is and she thought we were taking her there!

I said, "Mother, I told you Marg was meeting us in Jamestown and she'll take you with her to Minot." She calmed down, but didn't speak the rest of the way.

When we met Marg in Jamestown, Mother proceeded to tell her what a witch I was, but by then, who cares? I had been the heavy for two months and it was Marg's turn for awhile.

Marg got Mother settled back into her apartment, but since we couldn't get anyone to come in and take care of her, I had to look for options. None of my siblings wanted to take responsibility for the move, so, again, it was left up to me. I called all over and finally found a wonderful place that offers different levels of assisted care. They were new so they still had openings. All three of us girls were going to get together and move Mother in and make her home comfortable. But everything is such battle.

Mother really can be quite a snob. So when she first saw her new apartment she had a fit. It just wasn't as big as she was used to. It wasn't right. I said, characteristically, "Mother, you are being a snob. This place is beautiful and we'll make it nice for you!"

Mother cried, Ann scolded me for not being sensitive, and Marg treated mother like a nursery school kid, while giving me the cold shoulder.

Finally, we got the work done. We spent days hanging pictures, putting up curtains, and setting up furniture. She has a little kitchen, but is too confused to cook, so we only left a few things there. She'd had help with medicine, laundry, and meals, and all kinds of social activities. When everything was just right, we said goodbye. She waved and said, "Bye, Sweeties!"

I no more than got back to Fargo, when Mother called.

"Why am I here?

"What has happened?"

"How did I get here?"

She was hysterical. She had no memory of the past week. Nothing.

I explained to her that we had all gotten together to get her in a safe and comfortable home. That she would be all right. She settled down. Until the next day. She called.

"Why am I here?

"What has happened?

"How did I get here?"

This went on for about a week. Then, one day when I was explaining about the move, she said, "Haven't I always been here?"

I know it won't be long before there's another incident. But for the time being Mother is reasonably content. She is safe and has the care she needs. I'm more relaxed and my husband and kids appreciate that. They were very supportive, but it's hard to explain the pain you go through when you watch your parents decline.

I do know, though, it's strengthened me. It's caused me to be more introspective and really forced me to accept things *as they are* just because they *are*.

Chapter 4
Cynthia

I pull Reggie, my ten-year-old New Yorker into Cynthia's driveway and park next to a huge, sparkling, er – bread truck? A pickup, also gleaming, is parked behind, making me painfully aware of the acre of soil Reggie carries on his back, though I like to think it blends with his hip pewter coloring.

Cynthia opens her front door, which is a good thing, or I would have walked through the polished glass. She's striking and original, with a trim figure, highlighted hair, white-rimmed glasses. Bracing the front door with one arm, she lets me in, while she holds Clara, her velvety red dachshund, in her free arm. We bond instantly. Cynthia is nice too. A gnarled, rheumy speck of a chihuahua totters skittishly up to investigate. I am introduced to Sandy, whom I try not to frighten.

Cynthia invites me to sit in an airy white room just inside the front door. She and the dogs curl up on a couch facing me. The dogs sleep, though Cynthia graciously stays awake to tell me her story.

***

We're very lucky in some ways, Carol. My family is so close. There are six of us, and we all get along well. Everyone did the best they could with Dad's illness. My brothers and sisters here in North Dakota handled it all when we lived in Las Vegas, though we kept in touch by phone.

My mother's in wonderful health.

She's still living in Langdon. She's – she's a saint. Mom went through hell with my dad's Parkinson's. He was home and still farming with the help of my brothers, when he began having symptoms. He never did have any patience – but I remember when he first started having trouble eating. He couldn't pick up the food the way he wanted. He'd spill. Mom would tell him it was okay, that they'd handle it. But still – the frustration!

Eventually, the changes in his brain made him verbally abusive. He was just impossible to handle. Finally my mom called my sister Mavis and said, "I can't do this anymore." That's when they got Dad into Eventide.

Dad's deterioration was gradual and I guess I just denied it – Dad's being sick. I'd tell myself he was going to be okay. It really wasn't that bad. That he'd be better. But suddenly we were confronted with the very real fact that he was failing rapidly. We were still in Las Vegas then.

That's when Bill said, "Let's finish up our obligations here and go back." We'd thought about going back to North Dakota anyway, because of the kids. We felt they'd both have more opportunities in Fargo, but especially our son, who was getting into basketball. My sister Mavis got the kids registered at Roosevelt in Fargo, and we rented a house just a few doors down from the school. Bill closed up his business, I quit my job, and we moved back. My sister Judy was in Vegas, and she moved back at the same time.

I'll tell you, Carol, it was Godawful. I left a really good job in Vegas and Bill had to start from scratch here. We were totally broke. And Dad. Well, I know I didn't always handle all of it well. It was not good.

I was okay with the kids, but sometimes I was hard on Bill. And then Bill and I would sit up at night and say, "How are we going to pay this? How are we going to do this?" It put a lot of stress on him, and I had all that pressure because of Dad. Bill was such a help, but nothing could change Dad's Parkinson's.

Judy and I went up to Eventide twice a day, at noon and at six. We'd wash his face and shave him and trim his hair. We'd feed him. I put a lot of it on Judy, I know. I definitely couldn't shave him. I was still having trouble with it. Kids don't do those things! As tough as I am – and I really am a tough cookie – I just couldn't do some of those things for Dad.

Everyday when Judy and I would go down Main and turn on

Eighth on the way to Eventide, I'd get a headache. I just – it was just so hard. He couldn't talk by this time. His mind was excellent, until he froze up, but then he couldn't move, he couldn't tell us anything. Sometimes tears would well up, he had so many things to say. It was in his eyes. I know he was thinking, but he couldn't communicate.

I'm sure my family would have liked to say sometimes, "Why can't you just stay home?" A couple of times I didn't go with Judy, then I'd drop everything – Bill and the kids – and run off. Guilt. Either way. Guilt.

I'm the kind of person that can be happy one minute – go in the bathroom and cry – and come out and no one knows the difference. Bill and I could vent with each other – there were times, I suppose, when it wasn't good – it's just the frustration. Bill really was wonderful, though. Dad was a heavy, heavy man and totally stiff, and Bill would lift him. We'd bring him home in a wheelchair, and Bill would pull him up the steps.

One time when Dad was here he had a bathroom accident. I had to clean him up – it was just – I kept saying, "Oh, Dad, it's okay! Don't be embarrassed. I'm going to fix this!" I was just so upset, the only way I could get through it was to talk. I was so worried about how he must feel.

What really sticks were the silly times. We have a jukebox. Dad's favorite song was *"Wabash Cannonball."* One day Bill – he – he went out and got that record. There was one blank space on the jukebox. It was E-1. My dad's name was Ernie. Bill put the record in there and we'd play it for Dad. One day Judy and I hoisted him up and moved him as if we were dancing. We thought, "Well, why not at least try to have some fun?" We sang and giggled. Just silliness. But that's such a strong memory.

When Dad passed away, we were all there. Even my kids Emmett and Carolyn were there through it all. A lot of people thought that wasn't quite...the proper thing to do. I think it was right and really good. It was hard, but it was right for them. We were all there when the priest administered Last Rites. And I said, "Mom, look!" Dad was reaching for her. Then he died. All that time, he hadn't moved. I know all of this with Dad helped me when Bill's mother got sick. I had more compassion and more patience. I knew how hard it was for Bill because I'd been there.

One other thing I know and that is I don't want to stop my kids' lives. Someone else can take care of me when I get old. I tell them just to come and see me. If I still have my mind, I'll be worried about whether they got their laundry done, or whether they ate their peas!

That's all I want. Just come and see me. But let someone else take care of me.

Chapter 5
Bill

A cold wind has its way with my hair as I scurry through the rain and up the wooden steps to Cynthia and Bill's. That behemoth truck still sits sentry in the drive, glossy under the streetlights. I pull open the shiny glass storm door and knock.

Clara, the dachshund, barks. Then a young lady, who I knew must be Carolyn, their daughter, opens the door. She hangs on to Clara, and lets me in. At the sight of Clara I get sappy and silly, but after a proper tummy rub (Clara's – I didn't get one), I greet Carolyn, then Bill comes in to greet me. We'd met briefly when I was here to talk with Cynthia. As Bill leads me to his office, I ask about that truck in the drive. He seems amused as he tells me that it's his tool crib. He says it used to be a bread truck, but it makes a convenient place to store the tools for his construction company. Mystery solved.

Bill is medium height, with prematurely silver hair; a natural gentleman. He leads me to his office and offers me a chair by his desk. He's an engineer, quiet and understated. Cynthia's straight man.

Sandy, the chihuahua, comes in to check us out. She's more relaxed with me this time, even comes for a pat. I'm still kind of afraid I'll break her. Bill's voice is soft as he murmurs to Sandy, who was an abused wreck when they adopted her from the Humane Society. He pets her gently.

I ask about his mother, and Bill tells his story.

***

I'm originally from Wyoming, and my mother still lived there when she had her quadruple bypass. She'd moved into senior housing in Cheyenne, but didn't like it because she was too far removed from everything. Mom had a friend who did her shopping and errands so she was okay, but she liked to be where there was activity, so I moved her up here. We found her a place over by the clinic so she was nearby. She got to go and do the things she basically came up here to do. Mom went to see Emmett play basketball and watch Carolyn dance. She got to be part of the family action.

I took care of her groceries, her medicine, her doctor appointments. Actually, I guess that's when we discovered some problems. In order to maintain the medication she had – she had some hand tremors from Parkinson's, arthritis, and, of course, she'd had the bypass – I got her in to see a doctor. He found she had some internal bleeding. It ended up being cancer of the bladder, so over the course of time they had to scrape her bladder periodically.

Initially, she had office procedures, though she eventually had two surgeries. That disease caused her a great deal of pain. Then, at some point during her exams they diagnosed lung cancer, and also found symptoms of Alzheimer's. The progression of the Alzheimer's was kind of rapid. The dementia came and went, and she had lucid moments, but there were many times of disorientation and confusion.

I wasn't comfortable leaving her in her apartment, so I did some investigating and found out that she qualified for the high-rise across the street from us. We had thought it was just for younger people who were physically and mentally challenged. My brother was here visiting so we went and checked it out and we liked it. It had an elevator and so there were no stairs to worry about.

We were able to obtain a room for her on the eighth floor on this side, and she could look out her unit and see over here. I could even sit in our living room and wave at her. I could just walk across the street to see her, and we could wheel her across to visit, without having to get her into a car, which was getting difficult. They had alarms in the rooms for getting help, and a roll-in shower, which was great because she was having a lot of mobility problems by then.

At that point in time I started doing some checking into some personal care. I talked to the people at Eventide, where Cynthia's dad Ernie had been. They had a home care service, and we had them come in and help her. They even had someone to come and do her hair. At the same time, I arranged everything for nursing home care for a later date.

She was okay at the high-rise for awhile, but then she fell and was hospitalized. While she was at the hospital, she found out she was going to have bladder surgery again. That was when I called Eventide and said it was time for her to move and they found a room for her.

It was kind of rough sledding for awhile. She didn't like it. She didn't understand why she couldn't go home – she thought it was a motel and that the bill wouldn't get paid and she would be evicted.

Mom started on the lower level with the least care but within a month she had moved two more times, to two more floors, as she got progressively worse. She was then on the third floor with the people who had the most severe problems. During that time she had cataract surgery. They did one eye at a time, so I took her in for that. It had to be done because she was going blind – it was just like pulling a cloud over her eyes.

At that point, too, they were pumping her full of pills, vitamins and medication, trying to find the right one to treat her Alzheimer's. She had some adverse reactions, and the funny thing was, there were times when she knew that something wasn't right. That the medicine was wrong for her. Basically, I thought they could throw it all out, but eventually they did find one that seemed to help her.

They tried different restraints, too, like putting a tray on her chair, so she wouldn't get up and fall, but she just went nuts. She'd been free to do what she wanted for eighty years – and then to be cooped up – held back like that. She just couldn't stand it, so they had to quit that.

Then she did fall and break her hip. She was in rehab because of the broken hip, and her Alzheimer's medication seemed to be working. It was funny, she was really serene while she was there. As long as she felt she was progressing, she was great. She intended to walk out of there! She'd make bets with the gals – about how far she'd walk down the hall – how far she could go. It was a bunch of intense activity and she loved it. Then she reached a point where she couldn't progress anymore, and they had to quit the rehab. That's when she started giving up.

I don't know what it is about a person – but there's something inside that draws you. Comparing that to someone on TV – they have a look that isn't real. When my mother was here for Thanksgiving, I could tell. Something wasn't right. She had that look of distance – like someone on TV. I just knew....

Her life had gotten to a point where it just wasn't worth living.

When she knew she couldn't progress, she died. It wasn't until after it was over that I noticed how much it had taken out of me. You don't notice at the time, but...

I made sure that she could do as much as she was able. Yet, you wonder if you did enough. You always wonder. I do know it all really affected me – that I'm different somehow. I couldn't even say how, but I know it changed me.

Chapter 6
Julie

Julie and I are both apprehensive for about three seconds, but the common denominator of parental care dissolves the strangeness of distance as well as the distance of strangers. She is my buddy Jane's friend; an Atlantan, transplanted from New York state. I've never met her, but Jane's told me about Julie's struggles as she tries to care for her aging parents long distance. I'd love to fly down again, visit Jane, and meet Julie, but life has other plans, so we set up a phone date. Julie's manner is southern friendly, her speech New York quick. Listen with me as Julie tells her story.

***

I grew up in a very volatile household. Constant yelling and screaming. Mother and Dad fought all the time. It was very traumatic for us children. I have a sister and a brother. My sister was babied all of her life because she has health problems, but my brother and I have always shared responsibility, and still do. We really need to. That's the only way we can handle things emotionally. Living in that family was a real dichotomy though, because, through all the fighting and turmoil, my parents never missed a dance recital, or a program, never missed a kiss goodnight. There was a lot of love expressed.

Right now we're trying to get Mother into an apartment. She's on the list for low income housing, and they had an opening last week and she was going to move. She was all for it. Then she called and said she wasn't ready. It could be a year before another one opens up. So we're faced with that dilemma again. They have a bus, so transportation wouldn't be such a problem, and that would help wean her from driving, which she really shouldn't be doing. I would be so much more comfortable if we could get her settled there.

About Dad: I was a mess. The kids were a mess. We'd only been in Atlanta two months, and it was a difficult move for all of us. Anyway, just two months into the move, I got the call that Dad was to be operated on for colon cancer. God can have really funny timing. I was very resentful for awhile, until I worked through it and got my sense of humor back. Humor's always saved me, and I had to call it up this time.

I figure our parents brought us into the world. It's up to us to help them out of it. So I got my plane ticket and left. I had to think – who needs help the worst? My parents or my kids? From that perspective, I guess it was actually easier because of the long distance. I could say to the kids, "Here's my airline ticket – so this is really important." I had to kind of leave the pull of emotions out, and just go.

As I said, my parents fought all the time. But over these last ten years things changed between them, and they really had some good time together. Maybe it was their age. Or they just got tired of fighting. But their relationship seemed to come full circle. This was very healing for all of us. I think it kind of helped us all put the past behind us – it was almost God-given.

But now I was worried about how Mom would cope with Dad's being sick. I stayed on to help them through the cancer surgery, and could see they were doing okay. I did the legwork for setting up home health care and went home. I flew out a couple of times a year after that, but Mother took care of Dad at home for the next four years. The health care people couldn't believe what a wonderful job she did. She really worked at it.

She would get down, of course, and she would call me. Then I would get down. But when I'd call her the next day to see how it was going, she wouldn't even remember calling me. Here she'd been so upset, wondering how she was going to do this with Dad, and when I call she doesn't even remember!

Finally, though, Dad's dementia got so bad we had to look at nursing homes. I went and scouted out eight or nine, then narrowed it down to three. We decided that the first one with an opening was the one we would take. Then, they called from this beautiful new home and said they could take him! Dad moved in and they began a new phase of their lives. Mother visited every day. I became very good friends with the social worker. They were all wonderful people.

His care was excellent. I never saw any difference in the way people like my Dad, on Medicaid, were treated, and people who could pay on their own. The people there grew to love Dad and became Mother's support system. Dad needed around the clock care, and there was no way on God's green earth we could have done it.

Dad was only there a couple of months when he fell and broke his hip. I flew back out. He made it through surgery but then his heart stopped. We had a "do not resuscitate" order on him at the nursing home, but it wasn't on his hospital records, so they asked Mother what to do. She had to make an instant decision, and couldn't remember much, so she said they could ventilate him.

Then, when I got there, it was a big thing to get him off the ventilator, but, when we finally did, he started getting better. He did okay for awhile, but then started having trouble swallowing. The hospital said they were putting him on palliative care, and would send him back to the nursing home. He went back to die.

I decided it was time to make funeral arrangements. I picked out a coffin and flowers, got his suit cleaned, even picked out a shirt and tie....

When he got back to the nursing home, they asked why he was on palliative care. I said, "Look, we're not trying to kill the guy off! We love him!" The nursing home people said they thought the tests were wrong, and could they try giving him a little nutrition? We had a family meeting, said okay, and they started feeding him. He started getting better! I just went back and told the flower people I wouldn't need them and that I was buying him a TV instead. It was cheaper anyway!

You know, I've heard it from others, too. That generation of people from the Depression era – they're survivors. They're just so tough. It's remarkable.

When I got home, I thought I was just doing so great. But I got one of my chronic migraines and then had a stroke. After the stroke, I kind of thought I should throw my energy into taking care of myself.

Dad lived another year after that, though after about six months, he began to go downhill. Then he fell and broke some ribs. I kept calling, and was told he was doing okay, so I went ahead and left on a planned vacation to Florida. During that time, he had an episode where he turned blue when he was eating. He seemed stable, but I was notified anyway. He died the next day. I flew up for the funeral. Let me tell you, I was glad all the funeral arrangements had been made. That really helped when the actual time came. There wasn't an awful lot to be done.

I have to say, when I looked at my children and all the other grandchildren at my dad's funeral, and saw the grandchildren carrying the casket, I saw how life goes on. It was a kind of a beginning for me. I always thought that I couldn't deal with my parents dying. I wanted control, and death is the ultimate lack of control. But as we have aged – my parents aged and I aged – I have begun to understand that death is part of life's cycle. Dad's death gave me confidence that I could get through this. I think it will be harder when Mother dies.

Dad was an island unto himself, emotionally, so we weren't as close. Mother and I are pretty close. She's always sort of put me on a pedestal, and I've always protected her. So it will be hard. I will tell you this. When Dad died, he needed to go. I hope I'll feel the same way about Mother.

Marion Sandin Kelly & Wilkes D. Kelly

Chapter 7
Wilkes Finds Marian

Uncle Wilkes was a short round man with steel gray waves of hair, each doing as commanded, and a brush of iron mustache to conceal a short upper lip. He leaned toward ascots, silky shirts and tweed jackets, elbows patched with suede. An intelligence officer during World War II, Wilkes remained in government service throughout his career. He and Marian went to glamorous parties, entertained handsome people. And they came back to their native prairie once each year to visit us, their family.

When I was little, their arrival was a major event. We scurried around polishing the already polished, dusting the already dusted, anything to keep busy while we waited. Finally, they would drive up to our house. We'd drag in their bags with great anticipation. Once Uncle Wilkes opened his valise, anything could happen. Springs flew from peanut cans, gyroscopes spun across tables, Mom's new bottle opener mysteriously barked. My mother's sister Marian brought bags with quieter treasures: beautiful books from Old Williamsburg, a pretty pin, wonderful lace.

And when the adults dressed to go out to dinner! Marian, elegant in diamonds and fur. Wilkes, dapper in ascot and English wool. They were magical.

We children matured, Marian and Wilkes grew old. They chose to weed their possessions and move to Fargo. Mom and Dad found them an apartment in a nearby complex, and diamonds and furs, antiques and awards all made their final journey west.

While still in Washington, Wilkes had suffered a stroke and an aneurysm. Another stroke followed shortly after they came here. Then Marian collapsed. She had cancer, was operated on, and, in less than two weeks was dead.

A stunned Wilkes went home to be cared for during the day by home health workers. My parents, aging themselves, shopped for him and visited often. I did what they couldn't.

Soon, another stroke put Wilkes in the hospital, then Rosewood. My parents visited daily. So did I. Then Dad had brain surgery and he entered Rosewood. Mom and I played musical rooms, seeing one, then the other, now together, now apart.

Year followed year, stealing from Wilkes everything that mattered, but the most humiliating was the aphasia that stole Wilkes's ability to express himself.

"Fix my magazines!" he once shouted at me. I dutifully straightened the already neat pile of magazines on his table.

"No! My MAGAZINES!" He hollered, plum with frustration. I realized he couldn't find the proper word in his scrambled brain, and I started touching objects.

"Do you need new pens?" I asked.

"No!"

"Is your walker okay?"

"No! Yes!"

I opened his drawer.

"Your razor? Is your razor broken?" I asked. He looked at me like I was incredibly stupid.

"Yes. My magazines!" I got his razor fixed.

Uncle Wilkes was "The Colonel" at Rosewood, and had his chair in the lobby. His spot in the yard. And everything in its place. One resident, not pleased with my uncle's demeanor, insisted on calling him "Corporal." I'll spare you his response.

He began to think my mother was Marian and I was my mother, and he'd sit by himself, lost in the past shouting "Marian! Marian!" I wondered if he was hearing her sing one of the operas she had performed as a young woman. He seemed to be calling her back. "Marian! Marian!"

His blood pressure exploded. His breath wobbled. Early one morning they called.

"Carol, this is Margaret at Rosewood. Wilkes seems to be failing. You may want to consider coming down this morning."

"Thanks, Margaret. I'll call my mother, and we'll come as soon as we can."

I called Mom.

"I'll get the boys to school, and come and get you," I told her.

***

Wilkes lay waxy and still, tubes feeding air to his lungs as the oxygen concentrator hummed. Death clutched the room. Kim, the nurse on duty, assured us the concentrator would make him more comfortable, not prolong his struggle. I kissed his cheek, Mom squeezed his hand, we pulled up our chairs to wait, and, we hoped, comfort.

Kim came in.

"Colonel, I don't know if it will help, but we could try an antibiotic if you would like us to."

"NO!" Wilkes shouted with astonishing strength.

"Okay, we'll just keep the oxygen concentrator on to make you more comfortable."

We sat. I moistened the little pink sponge-on-a-stick and ran it over his tongue and lips. He nodded.

Gurgle. Gurgle. Gasp. In. Out. Gurgle. His breathing labored. His head bobbled up. Fell back. His lungs rasped. Then gurgled.

Drowning, drowning.

Lips crackling dry.

Furrowed forehead like windswept sands.

Please God.

Reaching. Reaching.

Let him die.

Reaching.

Grab her hand!

Lunch time. "You may as well go eat with Dad and tell him how it's going," I told Mom. She agreed.

Gurgle. Gurgle gasp. In. Out. Gurgle. Moisten lips. Stroke hand. The concentrator's mantra hovered in corners, circled the room, floated into the hall.

Mom came back up. Still we sat. Kim in. Kim out. Hold wrist. Check pulse. Nod. Whisper.

"He's slowing down. I don't think he is suffering too much," Kim said.

Holly, his primary aide, had come on duty. Tears swelled her eyes as she tidied up. She held his hand and whispered in his ear, then went to help another resident.

Kim in. Kim out. Holly in. Holly out. Check pulse. Soothe forehead.

Moisten lips.

Please. Just. Let. Him. Just...

Gurgle.

Die.

Cough.

Furrows smooth.

Peace.

Kim shut off the concentrator.

Dead silence.

Mom went down to tell Dad. I stayed. Waited for the official pronouncement of death. Memories reeled backward. The times I stayed with them in Arlington. After spring graduation. Before going to Europe.

I touched his cool plastic hand, left his room and walked to the elevator. The door slid open and two properly somber men pushed off a gurney with an empty body bag. I wished I'd left earlier.

I drove Mom home, returned to the empty room, stripped it of personal belongings, retrieved my children from school. Tomorrow I must deliver his uniform to the funeral home.

Chapter 8
Ann

Ann is sitting in her clinic administration office, studying her computer screen when I skulk into her office. The clinic is closed and I feel weird being here. "Hi, Ann," I stage whisper. "I feel like I'm sneaking around school after the teachers have gone home."

Her short wavy hair, the color of bronze garden mums, is brushed back from her softly freckled forehead. She puts her computer glasses back over her hair, and I wonder briefly how people do that. I tried it once and mine fell to the floor, popping out a lens.

"I've been worried about what I can say," Ann tells me as she motions for me to sit in a chair by her desk, "but then, it's your book!"

"I'll help you out if you get stuck, but I doubt that you will," I say.

I was right. Ann started telling me about her mother, and her story poured like water from the tap.

***

Maybe it was the makeup of my family that has always made it easy to put myself out for others. There were four kids in our family, the oldest was my sister, then the two boys, then me. I think by the time my parents got to me they just wanted peace. I think I kind of felt responsible for them.

Dad died in '83 so we've had Mother alone for a lot of years. My mother is an extremely negative lady. Extremely. I mean really negative! I hate to say this but she's not very loving – not fun to be around. She doesn't do "grandma things" or fun things so it's always been more of an effort to go to my mother's for the whole family. My husband says my sister and brothers don't go simply because it's not fun.

Well, it's not fun for me either. Mother has always had favoritism among her children. Always. She's basically very material. The more material success people have, the more successful they are as people. That's how they prove their worth. And, of course, that's why she thinks my brother in Detroit Lakes is so great. He has a good job and makes really good money. Never mind that he only calls her occasionally. When he does, he's a saint!

I don't mean to be entirely negative, myself. I love my mother... because she's my mother. I've had enough psychology to see some things. To ask myself some questions. I know that actually, I'm mostly glad that I'm the one doing all of the care even though I don't enjoy it very much. Do I enjoy the guilt of the other people? Could be. Maybe I enjoy feeling "better" than they are. Then I feel guilty about feeling that way! Actually I don't think they are aware enough to feel guilty.

I saw my parents' loneliness as their children left and they haven't seen this. If I'd been the middle kid or the oldest, maybe then it all would have been different. I feel like I've been with Mother forever.

Even before Dad died, she needed me. My sister, of course, being fourteen years older, moved away from home. Mother would assume I would visit her at her home whenever my sister came back. When I got there, I hadn't seen my sister for so long that we'd talk and leave Mother out of the conversation. Each time I would vow to myself not to let that happen again, but it does.

That kind of thing doesn't bother my sister at all. She really doesn't want to be left with just Mother to talk to, because it's too depressing. She'd rather talk to me. So, again, I'm the one who feels the guilt.

My brother who lives in Lake Park – the same town as my mother – helps her with some stuff around the yard and house. But his wife doesn't get along with Mother so they never have her over or do other things for her. My sister in Minneapolis just figures she's too far away to do anything, so she's fine ignoring the whole thing. And my brother in Detroit Lakes is satisfied with a few phone calls.

They know Mother is declining. They used to ask how she was

doing when they called me, but they've quit now. I sometimes wonder if they've just become accustomed to it, or if they're afraid of more responsibility – that they maybe should do something – so they just don't ask.

They got really upset when Mother accidentally threw away some old photos. My sister called me and told me, "Mother's done something with the pictures!" It was kind of, "Do something about it, Ann, it's your responsibility." I later worked it into a conversation with Mother, and she seemed relieved. She had just forgotten what they were and thrown them out. Sure, it was too bad, but it was an accident. She wanted to talk about it, but felt too bad to bring it up and my sister was just making it worse. She had told her, "How could you? They were pictures!"

The problems go back to way before Dad died. Mother had cancer surgery and chemotherapy here in Fargo. My brother would drive her to my house on Monday and his wife turned him into some kind of hero for this – his huge contribution. Mother would stay with me, I would take her for treatments, help her through the vomiting and pain, try to comfort her. It was so awful. But in all the weeks we did this, only once did my brother's wife take a meal to Dad, who was right there in town. And no one helped on the weekends when Mother was back home, still sick, knowing she would have to go back for more on Monday.

I don't know, maybe I haven't given them a chance. But we're getting too old to change. There's no use beating a dead horse. My husband wants me to confront them or quit talking about it, but I don't think that would do anything but make them bitter.

What I can't understand – does this not even cross their minds? That I have Mother for every holiday and am the one to check on her over everything? If I hear something in her voice when we are talking on the phone – some loneliness, maybe – I'll drive down on the weekend and surprise her. My sister and brothers tell her all the time they'll stop in and see her, but they don't do it. She gets her hopes up but it just doesn't happen.

They'll call me near Christmas and ask when I'm having Mother come to my house. She comes for every holiday, which is just as well, because if she didn't, I'd be expected to go to the place she visited and take care of things there. They can't manage being alone with her. It's easier here. She comes and we bake and I cook the way she wants me to.

Actually, I wouldn't have it any other way. I know that. It's just that I never dreamed it would have lasted this long. I always told my son that some day I'd show him the Christmas I really wanted us to have. Now, he's nineteen, and it's really too late for that.

There are lots of rewards in all this and I'm aware of them. People tell me I'll get my reward in heaven, but that's not why I do it. I do it because it's the right thing to do. And I'm counting on my son...! No – this will end with me. If I had a daughter, I'd be passing it on. Since I only have a son, it will end with me and my mother.

Chapter Nine
Janice

The front door is open, indicating to this stranger that she has found the right place. I knock on the storm door, and a tall (by my standards) woman dressed in soft red, with blonde styled hair, comes to the door and invites me in. Janice and Cynthia work together at the clinic.

Janice is welcoming and gracious. She asks if I'd like some refreshment, as she takes an overstuffed chair in her living room. I settle on one end of a mile long couch. Here is a woman who, after two years, is still passionate about the experience of losing her mother to dementia and death. She is articulate and occasionally teary. The prairie sun fades into dusk as Janice tells her story.

***

My mother got along well up until that last year and a half of her life. It was when she started having mini strokes things started to get bad. I feel fortunate we only had to deal with this for about a year and a half, because when you're in it, it's with you every day and every night. It never leaves you.

My kids were grown, so I didn't have young children to worry about. And I have two sisters. I don't know how people do it alone. My sisters and I lost our dad when we were pretty young – I was only fourteen – so we're very close. When something was going on with Mom, we'd all show up at the emergency room.

The mini strokes induced dementia in her. With some people, it takes an area that controls movement or speech. With Mom, it took pieces here and there of her brain, and that caused the dementia. She was in her own apartment at The 400 on Broadway, and at first, it was just the little things that you'd notice.

She started doing really strange things. Mom had worked as a cook in the hospital when she was younger, and she'd have to get up at three o'clock in the morning to get to work by five. Well, what she started to do was she'd call us about three o'clock in the morning. She would be so confused because she thought she had to get to work.

One night she called my sister. She said my husband and I had been in a car accident on the corner by her apartment, and that Larry was in bad shape and had been taken to the hospital, and she didn't know how I was. She said she had to get to the hospital. My sister called me at home, and I called Mom to try to calm her and tell her we were fine. She really didn't seem to be connecting, so I went over there so she could see I was all right. When I got there she was really surprised to see me and wondered what I was doing there!

We got more and more worried. The 400 is just down the street from Hardee's, where Mom used to like to go. And it's right by the railroad tracks, where she heard train whistles all the time. She was used to them. We were deathly afraid that she would decide to walk down to Hardee's, and a train would come by and she'd pay no attention. Or that she'd just wander off.

One of my sisters lost her husband a couple of years back, so she began to make excuses to stay overnight with my mother, and we also started having home care. At first someone came to clean a couple of days a week. Then we went to having someone come in a couple of hours in the morning to help her with small things and with her medication.

Each of us had our own way of coming to the conclusion that something had to be done.

For me, it really sunk in that Christmas. I said, "Next weekend, you come over here and we'll wrap gifts and things." Well, when we started wrapping, she really didn't want to have anything to do with it. I realized it was because she couldn't figure it out. So I said, "Let's do some name tags." It just hit me – Mom couldn't write out a name tag either! She was frustrated. She wanted to do something, so I ended up writing the name on a piece of paper and then she would copy it.

The month of January was pretty good, but then it went downhill quickly. We noticed that she would go into the bathroom and come back and have water splashed on her arms and her face. It turned out that she was afraid of the shower. She couldn't figure out the faucets and she'd get burned when she turned on the hot, so she didn't get in. She knew something was happening, and she kept trying to compensate so we wouldn't know. But it kept getting worse.

Mom grew up in the Depression and I suppose that's why she got so afraid that something would happen to her money. She got so she carried all of her money with her. We'd take her to the grocery store and just kind of let her go about her business. I remember one time we were at the checkout. I had been writing out her checks for her. This time she just took this big wad of money out of her purse and told the carry-out boy to take out that he needed! He and the checker both just stood there – they didn't know what to do.

Mom had problems with phone sales and with soap operas – thinking they involved family members – but the worst was the sweepstakes. When she'd get an entry, she'd think she had won, and wanted to fly out to California or down to Florida to collect her winnings. A lot of those old people get into that. It's really sad.

The more the dementia progressed, the worse the things were that she thought were happening. My dad died over and over for her. Family members were attacked. Everything she imagined was just horrible.

Mom had always been fiercely independent. Just fierce. The worst thing was... she said she never wanted to go to a nursing home. You knew that was just not an option for her. Yet we got to where we didn't have an option either. None of us was in a position to quit a job and stay with her. We started to take turns and spend the night, and she had help during some of the day, but we couldn't keep that up either. She got to the point where she couldn't be alone at all. We finally did have to put her in Eventide for her own safety.

I'd been trying for years to talk her into moving into their retirement home, so I thought a nursing home wouldn't be all that different. We all got together and said, "Why don't you just try it for awhile?"

We were fortunate that a room opened up, so we moved her stuff in. It kind of seemed okay until we were going to leave, but then the crying began. "Why are you doing this to me?" It was kind of back and forth, like she'd say it was okay, but when we were leaving, then she'd begin to cry. It was so hard to leave her there. It was just like leaving a little kid.

She kept having more strokes and she got worse rapidly. She didn't always know where she was. It got to the point where the room was her house and the hall was the street. One day when she saw me coming down the hall, there was this big flood of emotion. She figured now she had a ride home. And then I had to leave her!

Mom always liked to dress nicely. She was very conscious of her appearance. We tried taking her out to eat, but then when she'd drop food on herself – you wonder, should you reach over and wipe it off? How would that make her feel? And she would be so embarrassed to have food all over her. You just don't know what to do.

Then she fell and broke her arm. That traumatized her system, and she grew weaker. I was in a job transition then, and was to start a new job on Monday, so I was trying to get all this stuff done. Then my daughter called and wanted me to go to a rummage sale, so we did that. Her little boy was newly potty trained, and while we were in the car he said he had to go. I said, "Let's stop at Eventide. He can go there, and we'll take Grandma down for coffee."

A couple of nurses saw me getting off the elevator and hurried over and told me that Mom had fallen and they didn't think she would make it. Well, they took me to her room and she was gone. She had already died and they were trying to get in touch with everyone, but, of course, I wasn't home. They didn't want to tell me she died while we were standing in the hall.

They had taken her for a walk and she had just dropped. She was smiling and talking and then she was gone. It was such a shock! The whole thing – it's about the little things. You don't know how you're gonna do it one more minute. But then you do it anyway. And then suddenly, it's over.

I think I have learned to deal with death now. And I also know there are a lot worse things than death. To watch someone you love go through these changes. When they have no quality of life. That's worse than death.

I couldn't give up on Mom no matter how bad it got. I had to make her life as good as I could. Yet, I sometimes wonder if I did any good. But ...well, I couldn't just not try.

No matter what you do, you don't think you can do enough. It's always on your mind. I still – when I drive off in that direction – automatically start going to Eventide.

Chapter Ten
Roger

Eight fifty a.m. I have all my folks visited, their extras handled, and am expecting to meet Roger at nine. In his early forties, Roger, a paramedic, is of average height, slender, with short sandy hair. I'd seen him at the nursing home with his mother often enough to guess that he was the family caregiver, a role that's more often assumed by women, so I thought he'd have an interesting perspective. He, being the friendly sort, said it sounded fine and that we could talk.

Roger and I agreed to meet at Rosewood, since visiting there is obviously our major source of entertainment. Roger's father died there, and now his mother is a resident. As I wait, I explore the main floor, looking for an empty room. Saturday is a quiet day, and many rooms are locked, but I see the chapel is open and unoccupied. I wander out to the lobby, and see Roger walking in – exactly on time.

We pull up a couple of burgundy chapel chairs and sit next to the floor-to-ceiling windows. Sheer curtains filter snow reflected sun, giving the room a soft glow.

Roger tells his story.

***

I was the youngest of six kids. Dad was twenty years older than Mom, so when they got married during World War II, he just wanted to start having kids. And they did, until Mom couldn't take it anymore. That was Dad's personality, though. There were two ways to think, his way and the wrong way. He was terribly chauvinistic and had bad bouts of temper, so he was hard to live with. Mom went through pure hell to be honest about it.

We moved a lot when I was in school. Dad owned businesses in several small towns, and Mom worked in each one. I was the youngest and the older kids were expected to take care of me, but as soon as my parents left, we scattered. We weren't about to stay around the house all day.

I do think my being the youngest has a lot to do with my wanting to take care of everybody, and I have to admit to being a mama's boy. Mom favored me and let me get away with more. The older ones probably resented that, too.

Dad was basically a good man, a good provider. He worked 16-hour days and didn't have time for much else. My feeling is love 'em or hate 'em, you can't turn your back on 'em, so when he started getting sick I wanted to help him. He was in a wheelchair for years, because of arthritis, and then Alzheimer's began to take over. He had grown up talking Czechoslovakian and he began to talk Czech to people, and to call me Albert, his brother's name. Then he started having mini-strokes in his early nineties and with each one, he went downhill a little more.

Finally, at age 96, he had a major stroke. Here he was, confined to a wheelchair, having Alzheimer's and strokes. He was unconscious and we had to decide what to do. Dad's doctor had known him for 20 years and he knew that Dad wouldn't want to be left like that. They knew if he did recover – they had to figure what kind of a life he would have – the quality of it. My oldest sister is the very decisive type, and she knew he didn't want life support. Due to his advanced age, the doctors agreed.

But you know you can talk about it and have opinions. Well, you can change your mind in a hurry when it happens! It's just so hard to let them die. We'd sat vigil ever since they brought him back to Rosewood from the hospital. There were enough of us to be with him all the time.

But, you know – as long as we'd sat there – my wife and I had just stepped out when he died. I don't know, maybe that was the way it was supposed to be. It was probably for the best because it would have been so hard to see him go....

Mom had said for years that it would be a relief when Dad died, yet she's declined ever since he did. She's always been very strong and healthy physically, except for diabetes, and we saw her start to get unsteady. They'd lived in senior housing for years, and she had to change apartments when Dad died because she didn't need one that big anymore. After she moved, she quit senior volunteer work and began to really isolate. Then she began to get depressed and would fight going out when I went over on Saturdays. She'd talk about little things and get really weepy.

She never drove a day in her life, but she used to be able to take the senior bus service. Then she got so when she did take the bus she would forget where she was going and why she went there, so I finally said, "Mom, wait until Saturday and we'll go out and take care of it." I'd bring her the basics and her Sunday paper – she loves her Sunday paper – and then we'd shop for the rest.

A home health nurse would go over and get her insulin needles ready for her so she could inject herself, and they would check her blood sugar. They began to see that the blood sugar was all over the place and she wasn't injecting her meds right. She'd forget a shot one time and double up the next. The nurse said, "You guys, as a family, really have got to come up with something. She's going to put herself in a coma."

She really needed a nursing home, but she didn't have the money and the county would have to approve it first. It was just crazy. They had to get a panel together to make the decision and for some reason that was done in Tennessee!

There was so much time between when we knew she should be in a nursing home and when we could get it paid for; there was so much stuff to push through. She had to have a diagnosed illness so finally we got the doctor to do a CT scan. They said if it was something that could be treated, they couldn't approve her.

But they did find she had Alzheimer's. She really needed to be there for her diabetes, too. And she's got a ton of other medication. She has an Alzheimer's drug now too, and that seems to be helping her short-term memory a little.

She's been doing so wonderfully since she's been here. I see marked improvement. She's not so weepy, the depression has improved greatly. She's interacting with people. They've got her blood sugar under control. And she really likes it.

I've never seen this as a burden. I know I would feel awful if I lived away from here and couldn't get to town to help out. I think about it all week, so it's not just a Saturday thing. It's a natural part of my life.

When Mom's gone, who knows what I'll do? But for now, this is it.

Chapter Eleven
Diane

The warm, musty air takes me back to the old Carnegie library in downtown Fargo, where I spent half my childhood. And the late 1960's when I worked at the Patch Barracks-Vaihingen Library in Germany. And the late 1970's when I worked at North Dakota State University library in Fargo.

Diane is showing me the innards of the current Fargo Public Library, where she runs the shut-in program, and it's triggering a peculiar urge in me to grab a book and start collating. I keep my mitts off their property, however, and we leave the rooms and stroll toward Diane's office. Oooh so librarianish, with its orderly clutter.

Diane looks cool and efficient, as always. She's dressed in brown wool slacks, starchy white shirt, camel vest. I'm glad I left my jeans and flannel at home and wore khaki and corduroy.

She's a nice mixture of friendliness and professionalism, which I expect goes over as well with her program's volunteers as it did with my kids and me when she worked in the children's room years ago. After hearing about my book, she volunteered to share her own story of elder care. We settle into nice padded office chairs, and she begins to talk.

***

My husband and his aunt were always very close. When he was a child, he'd go there for lunch because they lived near the school, so they had a very strong bond. They never had any children, and my husband was the only male in the younger generation. There's a lot of sexism in people that age, and they just have greater confidence in men, so he was always special in her eyes, and we've made a commitment to taking care of her.

It's kind of interesting, though, that she insists on her brother having the power of attorney. He told us he's getting older himself, and really didn't want the responsibility, but we said he should respect her wishes and do it. We told him we'd help him. I write his business letters and my husband helps him keep up the rest. But that confidence is still there with her. She wants the oldest man to do it.

My husband's always been handy and his aunt has called on him throughout the years to go over and handle maintenance around the house. She almost has a hypothetical list for him of what should be done if something goes wrong. He goes over and fixes things for her or advises her when she needs a plumber or electrician. We also try to take care of her yard. She had a lot of pride in it, so we know how she wants it to look.

She'll soon be 90, and her wishes are that she will stay in her home until she dies. She cared for her husband there until his death, and she wants the same, so she has 24 hour in-home care. Hospice comes twice a week, because she's elected not to have radical treatment for the colon cancer that's returned. She had surgery for it years ago and when it came back, she said, "When I was much younger – in my 60's – I did it and it almost killed me. I'm not going through that again."

Our most difficult time now is around the holidays. I almost had a breakdown last year! The in-home care just collapsed. Even with 24-hour care arranged – it diminishes around that time. People take vacations and time slots can't be filled.

I told my grown children that we needed help with this. We just couldn't cover all the times. We took four-hour shifts and my husband and I spent the night. We were trying to have a Christmas celebration for our family at home, and spending nights sleeping on her couch or the floor, because we had to make sure someone was with her all the time.

The hardest thing to handle was her bitterness. She was very bitter about the upsetting of her schedule. She was actually mad because we were there instead of her usual people. I realize routine is so much a part of their lives, but we were struggling to take care of her, and to be treated like that!

It didn't help that I had injured my knee at work, and needed surgery. I found the floor at her house better than the couch, so I was sleeping there. About three o'clock in the morning she hollered, "Anyone out there?" I dragged up from the floor to see what she wanted. "Can I have some water?" She keeps a glass of water by her bed, but I went and got her some more, and then tried to get back to sleep.

I no more than fell asleep when I heard, "Do you think I could have some juice?" Then she was yelling, impatient because I was taking so long getting up off the floor! I got her the juice, and barely got back to sleep, when she hollered again. By then it was about five, so I just stayed up.

One of the caregivers who had left town on a long planned vacation was late coming back, so we had even more daytime to cover. My husband's aunt was furious. My husband had gone over to cover the gap, but she treated him like it was his fault. He finally picked up the newspaper and walked into the kitchen. She said, "Where are you going?" He said, "I'm not staying around when you talk to me like that."

We don't like to be like that, but sometimes, I guess, you just have to. Here you're trying to be upbeat and project a positive attitude – when somebody is bombarding you with this.

We are the generation that's trying to hold all this together. Our jobs, families, and caring for the elderly. For the last 20 years, his aunt has been saying, "I don't want to go to a nursing home. I don't want to go to a nursing home." But if this happens again, where the caregivers can't come for days – I don't think we can do it.

Even setting up home care was a nightmare. We finally had to go through two different agencies to get all the hours covered – which complicates the bookwork. We started having them all sign in when they came, and left instructions for medications and cleanup. That helped. And hospice is wonderful.

She has always denied being sick, just pretended she'll be fine and here she's being literally eaten up with the cancer. A nurse takes care of cleaning her, because she's getting so eaten up.

Thank God for the young man, the hospice chaplain, who went to visit her. Whatever he said – for the first time she came to realize she was dying and began to accept that. She's still bitter, but it did help. Part of it is that she doesn't feel the church has cared for her in her time of need – like they cared for people in the old days. The priests used to have more time to spend in people's homes when they were sick and they got all kinds of personal attention. It isn't like that now, and she feels forgotten. But this chaplain was able to touch her in a way no one else could.

She gives the nurses such a bad time. Pain management is what hospice is really good at, but she is so hard to manage. She says, "What do you mean? Are you trying to drug me? What are you trying to do to me anyway?" She denies her obvious pain and won't let the nurses help her. One who came to do her evaluation was nearly in tears. She said, "I don't know if I can keep coming back if she stays like this."

She can't get it that they want to give her a level of drugs to help control the pain, not to just drug her. She doesn't understand the difference. But she suffers more than she needs to, and that's really sad.

My husband always goes over twice a week, and we both go on Sundays. As soon as it dries up this spring, we'll clean up her yard and get it ready for summer. We'll keep helping her in every way we can. I don't know how long her money will hold out. This kind of care is a lot more expensive than a nursing home, and we get very stressed. But this is what she wants, and we'll do it as long as possible.

It's so hard for my husband. At first he was not accepting her condition. Finally, I told him, you need to deal with this now. Be angry, be upset. Grieve. But deal with it!

I think you really do some inner soul searching, when you go through times like this. You realize why you're here. This person has touched you in your life. You look at death and dying differently.

My husband and I need a certain amount of levity to live with this. I tell him if he gets like her, I won't be around! So we try to lighten the load. It takes great patience. One thing I do ask is – who will have the patience to be there for me?

Milton Bursack

Chapter Twelve
Remembering Milton

My father-in-law peered up at me, his blue eyes cloudy and weak, the right one a mere slit under its sagging lid. He grabbed his right leg with both hands and coaxed it over the ridge of the open car door, out onto the sidewalk. He inched his hips further to the right and struggled to place a second foot on the ground. I'd taken my mother-in-law, Alice, into the lobby of the clinic and pushed out a wheelchair, then set up the walker by the car.

"You're looking skeptical, Gramp." I said, "Don't worry. We'll make it."

"Well, Carol," Milton said. "I expect you'll get me in there somehow."

At five-three and a hundred five pounds, I don't inspire great confidence in people who need to physically lean on me. But Milton and I had done this before. He inched his two-hundred-eight pounds up, up from the car seat, grasped the arches of the walker for support, ducked his head to avoid a bump, rose up out of the car, stretching his six-four frame to as close to a standing position as he could manage.

"Okay, hang on tight and try to turn sideways." I told him. I pulled on the walker with one hand, steadied him with the other. He shifted to the side, then inched right, settling at an angle in front of the open door. The brittle air, at ten below, challenged his breathing. Thank God, the wind had relaxed.

"I'll bring the wheelchair up behind you," I said. With one eye on Milton, I dragged the still-folded wheelchair closer. Pushing on one arm of the chair, I pulled on the other, wrestling to get the thing open. Stubborn one this time. I wished they'd oil them or something. Finally, the arms spread and the blue canvas seat unfolded. I shoved the chair over a ridge of snow left by the blower and scooted it behind as Milton clung to the sagging car door with one hand, the walker with the other.

"Okay." I said again. "You can sit."

I heard the car groan - or was it Milton? - as he slowly lowered himself, cutting the length of his legs by a third, a half, finally letting go of the car, still holding the walker with one hand, grasping the arm of the chair with the other. I steadied his arm and tried to guide him gently into the chair. Thud. He was in. I put down the footrests and lifted Milton's feet to the supports. They only reached mid-calf.

I folded the walker and put it in the back seat. "Ready?" I asked. He sighed.

The chair wheel was wedged in the snow. I inched Milton forward, then back, forward, then back, while pulling up on the handles, then dragged it a bit to the side.

Leaning all my weight into the chair, I pushed Milton up the icy cement ramp, through the automatic door and into the lobby. Alice had been uncomfortable waiting in the lobby with a bunch of strangers, so she was glad to see us. I left Milton by Alice, skated back to the car, got in and drove it around to a legal parking space, then returned to the lobby.

I maneuvered Milton's chair toward the elevator, his legs sticking out like a forklift, only bumping into two pieces of furniture and one man. Alice followed. I punched the button, we waited two eternities. The elevator finally dinged.

There were three people on. Two got off. One man with a walker stared blankly and remained in the corner. Alice looked at me. "I don't want to ride on that," she said. "He's already got it."

"He has to go up, too, because we're on the lowest floor," I said. "Let's get on so we can go up to see the doctor."

I pushed Milton's chair forward at an angle, then dragged it backward and to the side so I could face him toward the front. It's the only way I could get his legs on with him. I wedged the chair in the corner opposite our friend who remained staring at nothing, then I stepped out and helped Alice on, placing her in a safe corner by Milton. "Isn't this cozy?" I said.

They both sighed.

I pushed the fourth floor button and we lurched upward.

The door opened, I helped Alice off. I got behind Milton's chair, leaned into it, and shoved ahead smacking his left leg against a wall, just a little.

Then I lifted and pulled the handles of the chair sideways and wedged around a corner toward the doctor's waiting room. We entered, registered, got coffee, and were called.

The doctor listened as Milton struggled to tell how weak he was, how awful he felt. The doctor told him he would have him take half of one medicine and double the other, the reverse of last time. As the nurse wheeled Milton out, the doctor told me once more, "He's wearing out. That's all. It's not likely any of this will help."

"I understand," I told him. "It's just that he feels so miserable."

I went to the waiting room, got behind the wheelchair and began to push Milton out. We went home.

Milton was my father-in-law and my friend. Before he retired, he was an optometrist, though he would rather have been an antiques dealer. We shared a love of words, classic literature, ancient art and architecture.

He spiced family meals with advice, as in, "I'll give you a little advice. You probably don't want it, but I'll give it to you anyway." His blue eyes twinkled. His chuckle rumbled. Milton held court. We listened.

To Milton, I was a little bunch of kindness, my poppyseed cake was tender as a maiden's kiss, and whatever rose above satisfactory was finer than frog's hair.

When Alice would go to her church circle, or shop for groceries, I'd stay with Milton. "Carol, go into the bedroom and get that triptych I made," he said during what turned out to be our last such visit.

I went in the bedroom and returned cradling the small triptych; three carved, red-painted, wooden panels, trimmed in gold, with a replica of the Madonna and Child inside.

"I want you to have that. Now be careful with it because the hinges are wood staples and aren't sturdy," he told me.

I thanked him and set it aside to take home.

"Now remember, the Nativity needs to be oiled with olive oil, at least once a year," he told me.

"I'll remember to do that," I said. He had brought the hand-carved set back from a trip to the Middle East.

"I polish the sterling Christmas angel you gave me," I told him.

"That's good," he said. "It'll stay nice that way."

He told me of a vision he had. Asked my opinion. We both knew we were closing up shop.

Not long after that visit, following our Christmas dinner, Milton went into the hospital, his heart failing, another stroke spreading through his body. I took Alice to see him. As we sat with him, Milton looked at me and said, "Carol, I'm afraid I'll be forgotten."

"No you won't," I answered. "Not with two boys carrying your name. You'll be remembered."

His eyes said he was satisfied.

Hours later, he was gone.

Chapter Thirteen
Shirley

History shadows me as I drive northside streets watching for Shirley's address. I grew up very near here, moving every few years farther north, the two-bedroom house growing to a three-bedroom house, then stretching to a five-bedroom house to accommodate my new sister, and eventually, my grandma.

A Minnesota Vikings flag snapping in the March wind grabs my attention. This is Shirley's. A grinning Santa stands in chunks of melting snow by the drive. A fat brown cat greets me as I exit my car, then Shirley opens the screen door, lets us both in.

Short, voluptuous, earthy, Shirley wears no make-up, a big shirt and slacks. An Easter village is on my left as I walk in. An egg tree, on my right. We walk past a highchair, waiting for an occupant, as we take a seat at the kitchen table. She's already engineered the quintessential grandma house.

"I was just putting on a pot of coffee," Shirley says.

"Thanks, but I've had plenty, Shirley," I say.

She laughs. "I guess I have too."

The cat, who insists on star status, is told to go downstairs. Shirley and I sit at her kitchen table as she tells me about her adventures with Mom and Dad.

***

Dad had been on medication for a long time, because he had these jumpy legs. He wasn't feeling well and we wanted him to have the dosage checked, but they wanted to see everybody on this trip they'd planned, and he said he'd go to the doctor when he got back home. He and Mom left my house and went to Burnsville, Minnesota, to visit my daughter.

Not long after, I got a phone call from my brother in Montana. He'd gotten a call from the Burnsville police, who were trying to identify someone with his last name. My brother said he didn't know anyone in Burnsville, but he'd called me because my daughter lives there.

Well, I immediately got in touch with the police. It turned out that Dad had gotten in his car and left my daughter's house without anyone knowing. He'd been picked up by the police for his erratic driving. They thought he was drunk. After they figured out that he wasn't drunk, they started calling around to find out who he was. I told them I'd call my daughter in Burnsville, because that was where he was staying. I told her, "Grandpa's at the police station! You need to go get him."

They went right down, with my mother, and took him to emergency. They found out his head was half full of blood and they couldn't figure out how he even drove like that. We all went out there right away, because they had to operate or he'd die.

When they operated, they left out a chunk of his skull, and just waited to see how he'd do. He was in intensive care, then. They decided later that there was more bleeding, and they operated again, and put back that chunk of skull. He came out of it enough to recognize people and could communicate some, but we had to find a nursing home.

I didn't feel my daughter should have to be responsible, so I found a nursing home here, in Fargo, that could take him. He was on a feeding machine when he went and we had been told there wasn't anything more that could be done, but when he got to the home, the staff there thought he could be rehabilitated, so they sent him to rehab, and he did start making progress. Even though he had aphasia, and couldn't think of the right words to say, he seemed to get better, and they took him off the feeding machine. Then we brought him to my house.

Mom and Dad had a house in Montana, so we sold that and brought all their furniture here. When Dad left the hospital both Mom and Dad lived with me. He had seizures all through this time. It was really horribly tiring. A home nurse came to bathe him and all that, or I couldn't have done it. I had to go to work every day and it was exhausting.

Then, right after Christmas, he had a really bad seizure. It took his speech and he wasn't able to move. He was back in the hospital then, and I said, "We can't do this anymore. We can't take him home." We found out that Rosewood had a room and I said, "We'll take it."

My daughter went up and did all the paperwork, you know, the stuff you have to sign about living and dying. I had just done all this with my husband a couple of years ago, so she knew it was just too much for me and she took care of it. My husband was young, so it was worse, but, still....

Dad went to Rosewood in January, and passed away in August. He had no life support. My mom spent every day with him, and I went two or three times a week after work. Mom continued to live with me.

After Dad died, Mom stayed. Then she had heart surgery.

She later fell and broke some ribs. All the time she lived with me, she wanted to go everywhere I did and do everything I did. It really got on my nerves.

I remember what you said one day, Carol, when you were in the store. We're used to them being our parents and now we have to make the decisions. That doesn't seem right, so it makes it extra hard. I try and remember that and be more patient.

I could get pretty mad at Mom. She always wanted to help with the dishes, but she wouldn't turn on any lights, and she never got them clean. I'd get mad and say, "Mom, turn on some lights!"

But I got so I could just not say anything, and wash them again later.

We tried to talk her into getting her own place but she said, "I'd rather be dead."

I said, "Oh, Mom, don't talk like that."

But she just wouldn't do it. She wouldn't get her own place. She went to live with my sister in Wisconsin for four months, and then went out to live with my brother in Montana. She was there for seven months. Finally, his wife said, "Grandma's really getting on my nerves. I can't do it anymore."

I totally understood.

It had been three years since Dad died. Everyone was doing their part, but Mom could be very demanding, and everyone needed their own life. So did Mom!

Finally, we talked her into moving into this little place in Miles City, Montana. We got it all fixed up. It's really cute. And now that she's adjusted, she loves it. She's back with her friends and she's learned to be a little independent again. She plays cards, exercises, and has her hair done every week.

It will be hard when she has to go into a nursing home. But I know I can't have her live with me again. My husband was sick so long. Then Dad. Then Mom living with me. Her surgery and stuff. I can't do it again.

I'm dating now, and would like a life. The man I'm dating is so patient with her. But when she's here, she wants to go everywhere with us.

I'd say, "Mom – he's not my husband!"

He says, "You'll be like that yourself someday."

I say, "No, I won't."

Then I catch myself saying something my mother would say.

Mom and I talk on the phone at least twice a week and I mail her a card a couple of times a week. So do the grandchildren. That way she gets mail, and she loves that.

I know I'm still angry with my dad – why he didn't go to the doctor? Why didn't I make him? We went to grief counseling when he died, but I still find myself thinking that. And I get impatient with Mom.

But after all of this, I don't let most things bother me so much. Before, if my house wasn't cleaned just before you came, I'd be all upset. Now I feel more like – life is short. Some things just aren't that important.

One thing I've learned from watching my parents is that if you don't do it now, you may not be able to. And I want to do some of those things now.

Chapter Fourteen
Mary

Tiny pebbles of sleet, bits of snow, and occasional splats of rain fling themselves against buildings and cars, reminding us that April in North Dakota can be an illusion. Yesterday it was 70 degrees. Tomorrow will be in the 50s. Today? It's all over the place. I regret wearing my winter jacket, but my spring one would be too light. These are the breaks of prairie life.

Zandbroz's lot is nearly full. I park Reggie, and ride the wind through the back door, where I'm greeted by a cheerfully painted floor welcoming me to Dakota Soda.

I glance into the soda fountain area and don't see Mary, so I have a perfect excuse to go into the main store. Aged wood flooring, rustic walls and shelves, dried flowers, and old jewelry hug visitors against the past. My favorite things, other than the books, are the wonderful handmade boxes. I have this thing about boxes, but we'll talk about that later.

"Carol?"

Mary pops out behind the old hats.

"Mary! Hi! I didn't see your car."

"I parked out in front. There's plenty of room."

"Let's go get coffee at the soda fountain."

Mary found a booth and we made ourselves comfortable. Mary, employed mother of five, tells the story of a devoted daughter.

***

About the time Dad retired, my parents sold their house, moved into an apartment, and then moved once more. Dad had suffered a heart attack a few years before their last move, and had quite a lot of heart damage, but he and Mom still had plans to do so much together. Then, one weekend, about six months after their last move, Dad woke thinking he had the flu. My mom couldn't get him out of bed and by noon she had called the paramedics. By 1:30 he was gone.

It was a horrible shock to all of us. I don't think Mom has ever really gotten over it. They had all these plans, and this was supposed to be their time together.

She used to be the one who had to coax my dad into doing things. Like their trip to Hawaii. They used some of Mom's retirement money to go. And after they got back, he was the one to tell people all about the trip. They had so much fun. Mom just sort of sat there, enjoying it all. The Hawaii trip was in January. Dad died in March.

Mom had developed late onset diabetes a couple years before that. She was insulin dependent and took good care of herself before Dad passed away. But after that everything started going kind of wacky. She didn't eat right. Like she'd go get a candy bar when she needed some food, instead of having a sandwich or something good for her. She just stopped trying.

At that time, I always had my sitter come in early for the kids, so that each day, on my way to work, I could stop in and see Mom. It was as good for me as it was for her. I had small kids at home, and a job, and things were pretty crazy sometimes. Just to relax for that half hour – it was so nice. She'd make us tea and we'd talk. My sisters would call her every day, too, and my brother was in the area then, and he'd stop by sporadically. So she had a lot of people checking on her.

Still, she just kind of steadily went downhill. Several times, when I went over, I found her in a diabetic coma. There were many trips to the hospital for that. And then once, when she really felt awful, we took her in. They hospitalized her, but couldn't find any problem except for some anemia. When that happened, we knew she needed more help, so we got her into independent living.

She was there for about four months, and then she was hospitalized with severe diarrhea. Her colon was inflamed from colitis. She wasn't able to go back to independent living because she was so weak. She was also diagnosed with Parkinson's, and the tremors had gotten so bad she couldn't give herself insulin shots. Rosewood had an opening so she went there.

It took her a long time to adjust; she had gotten so that any change was very hard on her. We also think she had a slight stroke during that time. Her personality – her attitude just changed so much. She'd always been a woman of such faith. But she's begun to say things like, "Why didn't they let me go?"

I think she's just tired of living. She really misses my dad so much. I say, "Oh, Mom, no." Her attitude – it's just that, you know, my mom – she's not the same person she used to be.

There was a time when she got a little better and we thought she could go back to independent living, with just some nursing assistance. But then – nope – she didn't want to leave Rosewood. I think she feels very secure there. And she's very attached to the people who take care of her.

One of my sisters handles her financial matters. And we all call and visit. I have one sister, though, who just can't handle visiting Mom in the nursing home. She has problems with the people who are in really bad shape. She calls Mom a lot, and when we take Mom to our homes, she sees her. But she doesn't go to Rosewood. And she feels really bad about that, but she just can't seem to do it.

Between my husband and I – we try to take the kids up on the weekends. We have five kids, and the older ones go to school close by and have often been over by themselves to see her.

There's always someone available in emergencies. Like, just this last little while, Mom was hospitalized again. My sister went up to emergency to be with her, because I had to pick up the kids. I don't have to worry that she'll be alone if I can't go, and that takes off a lot of pressure.

I used to do Mom's hair when she was home, and then, when she went to Rosewood, the volunteers started doing it. Lately, they've had someone sick, and another person on vacation, so they've had trouble getting everyone done, so I went back to doing it. I kind of enjoy it, anyway.

I go up every day, if I can. Some days it doesn't work, and Mom always understands. If one of my kids is sick, or something else happens, it's never a problem.

I take her to all her appointments, too. That's harder than it used to be. It's gotten so she's so slow now so that I have to go at least an hour ahead. She always used to be ready and waiting for me, but the Parkinson's has really slowed her down.

I can still take her in the car, but it used to be, if she was feeling pretty good, we could go out for lunch or go ride around. But now she usually doesn't feel up to it. I think it's the safety and security thing. She wants to go back to Rosewood.

And then she worries – she's had some accidents. One time she said, "I'll bet you never thought you'd be changing my diaper."

I just said, "It's nothing you haven't done for me."

I try to – you know – reassure her. I tell her, "There's nothing I wouldn't do for you, Mom."

No matter what has happened in our lives, my parents always stood by us. They weren't very strict when we were growing up. They kind of stood back and let us make our own mistakes. But they expected us to learn from them. I realize the sacrifices my parents made for us. Especially my mom. And now it's my turn – a kind of role reversal.

I think of all the kids in our family, I'll miss her the most when she's gone. It's part of my routine – my visits to her. I know there will be a void. I just feel like I can't see her enough.

I think doing this has changed the way I look at all handicapped people. I mean, I was always nice to them, but – well – this has made me more observant. I feel almost compelled to help people, like if I'm in a store and someone is having trouble. My compassion is more – developed. You just want to help.

Chapter Fifteen
Don

To me, being photographed is tantamount to labor pain. My old (since grade school) friend, Don, does everything to get me through it except encourage Lamaze. He says the puffing ruins my expression.

But today is okay. Don's not taking my picture, he's telling me a story. So I park beside McCracken Photography, a self-contained cube on north Tenth Street and walk in.

"Hi, Karen." I say to Don's wife. Karen is his business partner. My guess is that she also keeps things grounded.

"Hi, Carol. Donny'll be over in a minute."

As I take a chair facing the window, I see Don walking from his house across the street to his studio and up the steps. The sleigh bells attached to the door ring as he lumbers in. He's hot. We're all hot. The humidity is up and wild gray clouds are tearing up our sky. It's late spring, but acting like summer and soon rain will rip across the prairie, soaking farms and city gardens.

Don sits across from me and begins telling me about his friend Greg's mother. A woman who left an indelible mark on Don and his family.

Karen brings us coffee, and prepares to go back over to the house. On her way out, she stops, threads a few words through his, texturing here, smoothing there. She then goes off to some unfinished business, while Don spins his yarn.

***

When Greg and I were kids, if Greg didn't show up at home for supper, his mom, Bernice, would call over here. My mom would say, "Oh, he's already eating supper."

About a week later, my mom would be looking for me at suppertime, and she'd find me already eating at Greg's. We've been like brothers since seventh grade.

Greg's been working in White Bear, Minnesota, for years now, and makes it back here every few months. Since we're right here in town, we'd just continued being part of Bernice's family. She'd call us, oh, at least once a week. We'd call her every few days. But, you know, if more than a week went by without talking to her, we'd run over there.

She had a tremendous amount of pain – joint pain. And she did get tired of it. But she did really well. It was arthritis or something, but she was a very allergic person and they think she had pain and swelling from that, too. Still, she was very capable. She drove her car right up to the end – and she was about 85 when she died.

Oh, she was something! I remember when she had her double mastectomy for breast cancer. They didn't have to do radical surgery. We brought her home and she was so proud of the beautiful job they did. She said, "Just look at this!"

She pulled up her shirt to show us the great results. I just said, "wooww!"

She was a beautiful lady. Always very elegantly dressed. Prim and proper. She wore gloves, hats, heels – just always dressed to the nines. Bernice was also very outspoken. When she said something – well, she said what she meant and she meant what she said. If she didn't like the color of your shirt, she'd tell you. You always knew what she thought.

She would manipulate Greg, though, and she'd have had him coming here to check on her all the time, so we kind of filtered things so he only got called home when it was necessary. He relied on our judgment. He knew when I called she was having real problems, and he'd better get up here.

Mostly, Bernice got along well. She lived in a terribly nice apartment. And she loved it that Larson's Super Valu would deliver for her. All she'd have to do for groceries was push the security button and let them in. We never worried about her having food or anything.

She was so good to our kids, and they loved her. We had the

honor and pleasure of having her for each Easter and Thanksgiving. We were gone every Christmas, but Greg always made it up here then.

Everything was really routine until a week or two before she died. We were shooting a wedding out in West Fargo. She called the house and told DJ, our son, that she was in extreme pain. He told her what church we were at, so she called us there. I told her we were done and we'd pack up and be right over to get her. But when we got to her apartment, she had already left. It turned out that DJ had gotten so concerned that he went and got her and took her to the hospital. She knew that he was supposed to be somewhere, so she told him he couldn't stay, but he got her to the hospital.

When we got there, she was still very alert, but she was in terrible pain and was rocking back and forth on her bed. I said, "Bernice, what the hell is goin' on?"

The doctor came in then and said he thought there was some intestinal blockage, even though he couldn't see it. He wanted to give her two more enemas. He said, "Should they leave?"

She said, "No, this is my son."

We left anyway, of course, and I called Greg and said, "You need to get right up here." He said, "Is there time to get to my dental appointment first?"

I said, "The hell with the dental appointment, you need to get up here now!"

The enemas didn't do anything, so they said she might as well go home. They really couldn't see anything else. So we took her home. We had to get back to do the wedding dance. She was home for about an hour, and she called a lady in her apartment who took her back to the hospital. Karen called Bernice's apartment from the church to see how she was, and found out that she was back in the hospital. Karen went right away, while I finished up work. Greg got there, too.

Finally, I was able to go. Bernice kept complaining about the pain in her intestinal tract. It was excruciating. She was in a really nice room, and they were doing what they could, but nothing helped.

She said she wanted to die. She was ready.

Actually, she had been ready for quite some time. We'd talked about it a lot even before she went in the hospital. She said she just hoped there wouldn't be pain when she died. I said, "Look, Bernice, when your mother died, I was holding her hand. She had a beautiful, peaceful look. It was a great moment. There was no pain."

I want to say, though, that she was always very much in love with life. It's just that she was 85 and tired of pain. Her mind – she would recall everything, from her father plowing with the horses to what happened yesterday. She remained sharp and in command. But, now, she wanted to die.

We had gone back to work. Greg and his foster sister, Margaret, stayed with Bernice. Then, she just suddenly died! That was it. The sack around her heart filled with blood and she was gone. It was peaceful. Just like I told her. No pain.

Bernice gave more to us than we ever gave to her. We just helped when we were needed and enjoyed her company. She was a great lady.

Chapter Sixteen
Emily

It used to be Randy's. Then Broadway Junction. The name keeps changing, but after I push through the double entry, everything seems pretty much the same. The hostess offers to show me to a table, but I tell her I'm waiting for someone, and sit, instead, on the grape vinyl bench by the door.

Through the window, I see Emily drive up, park, and hurry in.

"Hi, Carol," she says.

"Hi, Emily! It's good to see you."

We walk over to the hostess sign and wait almost a second.

The hostess balances a giant jar of broccoli on the edge of the salad bar and comes to take us to our seats. We choose a booth by the large windows facing Broadway. The traffic is sparse this Sunday afternoon.

Baby boom gray weaves through Emily's pale blonde hair, catching light from the east window. Her blue eyes are soft and cheery, as you hope the eyes of a nursery school teacher would be. She's smiling, and I sort of expect her to give me a sticker.

Instead, Emily tells me about fourteen years of parent care.

***

I grew up in Crookston, Minnesota, but moved to Fargo when Scott and I were married. My sisters and brother are scattered all over the area, but we stayed closer to Mom and Dad. They liked Scott and I was always concerned about them, so it was natural I guess.

It wasn't too long after I moved here that my mother started to get sick. Her mind was sort of going, and she just really couldn't function. Dad always prided himself on taking care of her, and he did, but he needed help, and that's when our fourteen-year, twice-a-month drive from Fargo started.

Dad was determined that Mom would never go into a nursing home, and we struggled to make that possible. We set up 24-hour care, which actually wasn't always that good. Oh, near the end it was, but at the beginning, we had an agency do Monday through Friday, and some private people do weekends. We weren't happy with that, so eventually the agency took over the whole thing.

It went okay after that, I guess, but Dad was failing, too, and he just wouldn't give up. Sometimes I think it would have been better if we'd just gone in and put them both in a home, but you try to do what they want.

I guess it was all worth it, because Mom died in Dad's arms, and that was very important to him. I doubt if she knew where she was, but they were very close, and it was probably best that way. The agency kept coming to take care of Dad, but Mom's death really affected him and he started going downhill fast.

My siblings wanted to keep Dad at home as long as possible. I understand that, but even though they were good about going to see him – and they did a lot – I think they don't realize how hard it is when you're the one that all the responsibility seems to go to. The one arranging everything, getting all the mixed up and angry phone calls at night, driving every couple of weeks, giving up this time with the kids.

I felt like I was the mother for so many years – with both my parents. It's something people don't understand unless they've been through it. You have to make decisions for them, when they used to make decisions for you.

I know when we made Dad give up driving, it was so hard on him. We finally got the doctor to convince him that he had to stop. It had to be done, and probably should have been done earlier. That was probably the worst.

Dad had been having mini-strokes and his personality changed dramatically. He became a completely different man. He was very strict when we were growing up, and I never did stand up to him, but this new personality was much more difficult. Then he began falling a lot, and the person helping him had to call for help. It just became too hard for them so we had to look for a nursing home. He was so in and out by then, that I don't think he cared. One of my sisters kind of fought it, but we all ganged up on her, and she finally came around.

We found a place in Ada, Minnesota, still quite a drive for us, but it could have been worse. And one thing about it being in a different town, you could go for a visit and then when you got home just sit and cry for awhile, not knowing when you'd be going back. Or maybe because you knew you were going back?

It was okay for a couple of months, but then we got the flood. We'd had that ice storm which had taken down the phone lines, and then the ice jams after that record snow. The river came up so fast – they suddenly had to evacuate. All those old people had to be scattered around the area, and separated from each other and their nurses and aides. We kept trying to find out where Dad was, but phone lines were down all over. I don't even remember how it all went – I've kind of blocked it out – but I remember we went out and bought him some clothes. I didn't even know if he had his false teeth!

Then we found out they had things under control, and had supplies for people – and he had his teeth. Everyone was so caring. They felt really bad about what happened to these old people. The Red Cross and Salvation Army were wonderful.

As soon as I knew that the home was lost to the flood, I called a couple of places in Fargo to look for a room for him here. I got a call back from Rosewood that they had a room and I had to decide on the spot to take it. I hadn't even been in the place for years, not since it was called the Fargo Nursing Home. But I knew I really didn't have a lot of choices, so I decided without talking to my husband or anything. When I went over and looked at it, I was so pleased. It was homey and beautiful. That was such a relief!

We had Dad moved by a handicap service. They brought him to Fargo, and he stayed at Rosewood until he died last year. It was nice having him in town. No more driving! I could go up two or three times a week, stay for a couple of hours and go home. By that time he was getting so he didn't respond much when I did go.

Sometimes I don't think he even knew I was there. But I found out my visits really did matter when they had that flu outbreak last year. They wouldn't let visitors in for ten days. Of course, when they said I could go back up, I did. When I got off the elevator, I saw they had him in a recliner in the main room. I walked to him and he held out his arms. He just lit up! I knew then it all made a difference.

I'm glad I did it for both Mom and Dad. But there are times when I wish my brother and sisters could have been there more, maybe just so they could understand....

At least when he did die, two of my sisters were able to be here with us. A nurse asked us if we would like to call a priest or minister, so Scott and I decided we'd better call everyone and tell them he probably was going to die. Two sisters could come, and then we called our minister and he came and we all had communion. I'm sure it didn't matter to Dad, but it was good for the rest of us. When the minister left, Dad seemed relatively stable, he seemed to be resting peacefully, so we decided to go get something to eat and come back.

He died while we were out. We went right back, but he was gone. Sometimes, I wish...well, I would have liked to have been there to hold his hand. He was there when Mom died. But maybe it would have been too hard. My husband said it was better for me that I wasn't. The nurse was wonderful. She was so comforting.

I certainly understand more about the elderly and loneliness after having gone through this. I think I learned to put up with a lot more, too. Being part of this really makes a person think. Will someone take care of us?

Clarence Bradley

Chapter Seventeen
What Happened To Brad?

Dad was agitated. I could tell by his jerky movements, his flushed skin. He was perched on the edge of his lift chair, shuffling though a pile of papers on his knees, some of which were spilling onto the floor. A table on his left was covered with sticky folders and curled, spotted business papers. Three overstuffed brief cases and a file gaped open, more papers crouched under the sink and huddled under his chair. Juice-soaked business cards stuck to the wheeled table on his right, joined by his candy basket, call-light and tissue box. He looked up hopefully as I walked into his room.

"Good. There you are," he said. "I need you to...to...take some, uh, some, dic...oh...some dictation."

I caught a sigh before it escaped and replaced it with a smile and breezy attitude, as I kissed him hello.

"Sure. I can do that anytime. How are you?"

His eyes were red and unfocused, the look of his very delusional phase – as opposed to his somewhat delusional phase. My mission was to tame the tigers in his brain, so he can relax for a time.

"What I need is a list. The city commissioners. A list of them because of the elephants. I need you to write a...oh, a...a...you know what I need, just write a...a...pro...pro...."

"A proposal?" I ask. "Sure, I can write a proposal. You want the commissioners to get an elephant for the city?"

"We've been working on it," he answered. "But no! Not the...not the commissioners, but I've been working on...I've been asked... they've asked me to get an elephant and be a part...."

My brain searched for answers as it tried to separate the scrambled images Dad was relating. I got out the yellow legal pad he keeps by his chair, and began taking dictation. His fingers are numb and his eyes, ears, and brain are marginal, but tools for his work he must have.

"We are getting a new zoo, which is no longer a city project, but there is a zoo board. I'll bet you're working with *them* to bring in an elephant," I said. I was beginning to feel the effect of endorphins, a feeling that I could go the distance this time. I wrote – *elephant.*

But then.

"And that Catholic prayer...the one that repeats...repeats... Mary...something, bring me that. I need that."

Considering our Presbyterian heritage, that was an unusual request, but, after six years of this, I am rarely surprised.

"Oh, you mean the Hail Mary?" I ask. "Hail Mary, full of Grace? The one they say for the Rosary?"

"Yes! Yes!" he answered, looking at me as if I truly had lost my mind this time. "Yes, why do you ask?" he said.

"Sure," I said, grateful for the Catholic friends of my childhood, and my dear Catholic friend Jane, who taught me that prayer. Dad had raised exotic ants between windows, kept bees (who wintered in our garage), dug for fossils and scoped out the planets. In context, his need to bring an elephant to Fargo, or to have the words to a Catholic prayer were mundane.

I wrote - *Hail Mary.*

"And the names of the commissioners, and their phone numbers and the addresses and where to put the elephant," he said.

I wrote - *list commissioners.*

"Okay," I said. "I'll have the zoo board contact you about the elephant, type up the Hail Mary, and get a list of commissioners. Will that do it?"

"I think so. Yes, good. Yes, that should be good," he said.

His color improved, the agitation slowly drained away. My jaw relaxed and I breathed more easily as I realized that today I'd won. Just for today, I had quieted the chaos.

How to proceed in filling his needs for tomorrow? The Hail Mary, no problem, I know it and can type it out. The commissioners, no problem. In fact, I'll get him the meeting notes off the Internet.

But the elephant and the zoo. A little challenge. I'll have to write a letter from the zoo for Dad, thanking him for his interest, and inviting him to help them in the future when they are ready to bring in the elephant. Shouldn't be too bad. Easier than the letter from the military thanking him for wanting to be an officer, or any of several letters from our mayor. I really should let the mayor know about the letters he's written Dad. Some other time.

Dad's given name was Clarence, but he was always known as Brad. He was a retired city employee, growing old, a bit confused, but still Brad. Fluid had begun to build up in the scar tissue left behind from a closed head injury sustained during maneuvers in World War II. Dad, the skinny, fair fellow whose ancestors thrived in cloudy England, collapsed while training in the Mojave Desert, smacking his head against desert rock. He was in a coma for weeks, then spent months in rehabilitation, learning to walk and talk. He fought through hell to lead a normal life, working, fathering two more children, getting a degree, holding the position of supervising sanitarian for the city of Fargo.

But as he grew older the injury began to haunt him. His waterlogged thinking would grow worse if he didn't have a shunt put in his brain to channel off the fluid. Specialists recommended the operation.

Surgery day. As they wheeled him away, he forced a smile, thumb and forefinger creating a circle signaling "okay."

Hours later, we faced a sleepy man. We were filled with hope.

Days later we came to realize Brad had gone to sleep on that operating table and Clarence had awakened, firmly bonded with a voice in his head we came to call Herman. My dad, as I knew him, was dead. We were filled with despair.

Our family soldiered on. Since that time, I've created degrees he thinks he's earned, designed awards he thinks he's received, written letters he thinks are coming. A few loyal friends still struggle to visit him, but it is so distressing that most stay away. Clarence is a bit frightening, and they want to remember Brad.

One morning blood pressure and pulse barely there, he's Rip Van Winkle. Another morning, bright-eyed and mischievous, he's Dennis the Menace. He can be a great musician, a military officer, a doctor, lawyer, or president of the United States.

Dad was born prematurely in 1917. He's been hospitalized for pneumonia twice and nearly died from a penicillin reaction. He survived a closed head injury to claim the life God promised him.

So what are a few elephants? I'll see what I can do.

Chapter Eighteen
Elaine

The Fryin' Pan. It's one of those places filled with regulars who the waitresses know by name. I told the hostess that I was meeting a woman shortly, then took a seat in the nook set aside for waiting.

A fellow walked up, handed me a *USA Today* and said, "Here's something to read."

He plopped on a western style hat as he walked out the door whistling.

Nice of him, I thought. I glanced at the paper, but spent most of my time watching people out in the Main Street parking lot. Elaine drove up, jumped out of her car and hurried in, looking a trifle flushed. I met her at the hostess sign.

"Hi, Carol. One of those days."

"No problem, " I tell her. "I've been enjoying the people."

After ordering coffee and discussing important hair issues, we get down to business. I know Elaine lived in the same home as her in-laws for seventeen years, and I'm interested in hearing how it went. Elaine shares her story.

***

We'd been living in Wisconsin and really enjoying our lives, Carol. There were a lot of close friends, and we had wonderful neighbors. But when my father-in-law, John, started getting forgetful, I said, "Maybe we should move back there."

My parents were in Fargo, and my husband's were on a farm north of there. I knew they'd have to leave the farm unless someone was out there with them. So we decided to make the move.

It took about a year to get things arranged, and we had to take a big cut in pay, but we did it and moved from a large city environment back to the farm. Anyway, we started out with a small story-and-a-half farmhouse, and added on to it. We built a family room as a shared room, and then a kitchen, bath and bedrooms for my in-laws. For several months, while all the building was going on, we lived together in the main house.

Our boys were in first and fourth grade. The move changed a lot about school for them – going from such a large school to one where there were a total of a hundred kids. The first grader did very well, especially socially.

The fourth grader was a terrific student, but never adapted well socially. He was the new kid in the class when he started, and he was the new kid in the class when he graduated. But maybe it would have been that way in Wisconsin, too. Fortunately, they had each other, which was important on the farm. They were very good friends and did a lot together. And they always enjoyed having their grandparents around.

I cooked all the meals when we all lived together, and my mother-in-law, Grace, cleaned up. She baked a lot. It went fairly smooth. I did most of the clothes, as I remember, but she helped clean. She is just so nice, it never was really bad.

The whole situation was hardest on Grandpa. He had always dominated his household. When my husband started calling the shots, it was tough on him. But that got better with time. He never said much to us, but I'm sure my mother-in-law heard about it – like how we raised the kids and other things we did that he would have done different. I don't think she had it easy with him, but it was all she knew. Grace was always smoothing things over with him, and she was easy for us to be with, too.

Eventually, the house was done, and they moved into their own apartment. They had a door to close for privacy when they wanted it. They were never intrusive or interfering. She just loved watching the kids grow up and she loved being a part of it all. My friend in Wisconsin had said, "I'll give you a year."

But it really was okay. She was just such a good mother-in-law!

John was getting more and more forgetful, though, until eventually he had a bad car accident. He was driving around and couldn't remember where he was going – got mixed up and totaled the car. Grace was taken to the hospital for observation overnight, and he kept saying he'd killed her. That's when he finally quit driving. She never did drive much, so I became their wheels.

Really, his right arm was Grace, though. She took care of him totally then, except for the driving they needed. I took them to doctor appointments and anywhere else they needed to go.

Eventually, I began working in Fargo part time. And really, they didn't need a lot of care for the next six or seven years. Just the driving. But then the hardening of the arteries got so bad that he wasn't recognizing people, and he had to go into a nursing home. He went to Elim and was there for 15 months. By then he was really quite mellow. He didn't know anybody or really know what was going on much. We took him home for Christmas and his birthday, but, it was like – he was so frightened. You know, all these strangers around.

One day they called and said he was having some distress. We all went in to see him. Then he just slept away.

Grace was very religious – not with a lot of hang-ups or anything – just deep faith. That helped her through that, and a lot of things, I think. She continued to live in the apartment, but she did most of her own cooking and was pretty independent.

But then the dog died. This dog had been around for about sixteen years. I don't know if she thought she needed to stay to take care of the dog when no one was home, or if she felt the dog was taking care of her. But when the dog died, she decided that it was time for her to move to a retirement home. Just like that.

We ended up checking a lot of places, but she moved into the Fairmont. And, you know, she never seemed to care that she was leaving us! I was so sad, but she was all ready to go.

They were wonderful there, but she didn't get out of it what we had hoped she'd get out of it. She had a severe hearing problem and was getting paranoid. For instance, she'd hide her hearing aids and her key because she thought someone would steal them. We went about three times a week to see her, and we'd play hide and seek trying to find her stuff. She'd hide them in the lamps and everywhere else imaginable. She was very crafty.

She also got to the point that she wandered. One time she thought there was a wedding, or a funeral, or a shower or something she had to get to, and she was worried she couldn't get there so she started out walking. They caught her twice down the block, and they told us she'd have to look for another place to live. They were very kind and they watched over her far more than they were obligated to, while we looked for a place.

We got her into The Evergreens. It wasn't a full care area, but she was in a memory loss section. That place was really the Cadillac of homes. A fantastic arrangement.

They had a code you had to punch to get out the door, and I remember people asking me how I got out. And I'd tell them, "Oh, I forgot what I did!"

Grace's mental state kept deteriorating, and she started to have accidents. She walked with a walker, and she started falling because she'd get up and start walking, and forget to use it. She also needed help dressing. We decided it was time for a full-care nursing home.

We made a bad mistake when we moved her. She had no memory, at least not over five minutes, so we didn't tell her ahead of time that we were moving her. I mean, she was always seeing her husband or seeing her folks; there was no reality there. But the people at the home didn't know we hadn't mentioned the move yet, and they brought it up in conversation.

When we went to get her and told her we were going to take her to a nice place – that's when we knew we should have prepared her. We took her over, and got her settled – we thought – and then told her we had to get to work.

She said, "You can push me or shove me anyplace you want."

We just felt awful.

She's fine now, though, even quite humorous. Her dementia is bad, but she feels okay. She did flush her hearing aids down the toilet or threw them out or something, but otherwise everything is going okay. Actually, this is the easiest I've ever had it. The moves were hard, but we know she has good care and that's great.

My husband and I have both had this virus and haven't been able to go up for awhile, and that's been a problem. I felt so guilty, I even talked to a social worker. But he said, "You can't be putting a guilt trip on yourself when you can't go. You are doing the best you can. Let the guilt go."

It helped to hear that. So, we'll go when we can.

But I was always the main caregiver, and not to see her every day – and I was her wheels, and her ears – at the doctor and all the other things...we were very close. You know, she told someone at The Evergreens, "We were living together for 17 years, and we never had a fight."

She's right.

Actually, I think the move back to the farm, even though it was an adjustment, was to our benefit. I was really a Type A. I mean really. I've gained patience and a lot of perspective about life from it all. And, when my own Mom got sick and died from cancer, I was able to spend whole days with her, since we lived here. I wouldn't have had that time, if I hadn't moved back. I've just learned to appreciate the way life works a little better. I think it's been good.

Chapter Nineteen
Merrie Sue

Some of my favorite spots around Fargo-Moorhead, especially in the summer, are our college campuses. We're blessed with three – two state universities and one private college.

Elegant trees in full dress, velvety slopes of clipped grass, abundant gardens wild with color thumb their noses at memories of winter snow. Art students sprawl on lawns, sketching; architecture students survey; horticulture students tend new hybrids; stuffy professors air out their personalities.

I stop by Merrie Sue's house to get her and we drive over to the Minnesota State University Moorhead campus for coffee and conversation. Inside the maze of hallways leading to the student lounge, we choose a little table by a window looking out on a lush atrium. Burgundy peonies wave from a far corner.

Merrie Sue and I met when I wrote some pieces for *The Area Woman*, a local magazine where she's managing editor. She also raises children, teaches at Concordia College, is taking some classes at MSUM, teaches baton. And yes, even though she's well into the baby boom years, she's cute and perk...uh, vivacious.

Merrie Sue has a story to tell.

***

I think my mother – her name was Elberta, but everyone called her Berta – just denied her cancer to herself when she first discovered the lump in her breast. She had taken a friend of hers to Mayo Clinic for her regular cancer treatments and she saw what it was like. She just didn't want to go through that. So, when she found the lump, she seemed to deny it for awhile, and then made the conscious decision to die. To not go through what her friend did.

I don't think, anyway, if she had told my stepdad – at the time – that he would have been supportive. He may even have been angry; made her feel it was her fault.

My dad had died suddenly of a heart attack when I was thirteen and my mom married Al when I was in college. My brother was still at home, so the remarriage was a lot harder on him. Al was a road salesman, gone all the time, lots of eating and partying. He had a sometimes abrasive personality, and could be hard to live with.

Mom had tuberculosis when I was three. She had to go to a sanatorium for awhile, and I know she received a lot of powerful medication when she was there. I kind of suspect that those massive doses of chemicals may have played a part in her cancer. And then, she was a beautician for years.

She used to say, "The only thing in life that's worth having is a good haircut."

But all those old chemicals and dyes they used. It had to have an effect.

She found this lump. I didn't know about it at the time. I was 14 hours away, living up near Minot, and busy having babies and living my own life. But finally we could see there were problems.

She was saying, "I've got a bum back. I've got a bum back."

So I went down to southern Minnesota to see about this bum back. By then she was using a cane and a walker, and she still hadn't seen a doctor.

I saw bandages and other things around and thought, "What the hell is going on?" By then, she was in her mid-sixties. She finally went in to see the doctor when I was there. I'm sure it was a relief. She wouldn't be alone with it anymore. It was the doctor she'd had forever, and she finally had it out in the open.

They showed us the x-rays, and there was a spot of cancer on the spine. She had little spots of cancer here and there. But the one on her breast - ugh. Yuck! It was eating her. The funny thing was, after all these years of smoking, her lungs were clear!

We were still living 14 hours away. Mom wanted to be home as long as she could. So we got home health care to come in and the doctor gave her some pain pills and sent her home. I had stayed – we were doing the Amtrak thing then – and my family had gone back.

Within two days, mom was losing her urine and was just – just out of it. I think the medication may have had something to do with that. She'd just – pee. She couldn't help it. And she was in pain.

That night I knew I was going to have to tell her she needed to go to the hospital. I remember – I went to see "Man of La Mancha" at the high school that night for diversion. But mostly I just paced outside all night. I felt like I could throw up any minute. Just – ugh! You know the feeling.

I called her pastor and said, "You have to tell her!"

So he did. He said, "Berta, we have to get you into the hospital." And she went. I think she was so out of it she couldn't argue.

They came to get her in an ambulance. You know, in a small town – she knew all the ambulance people. Tears. There were tears. It was hard on them to see her like that.

Here's a question for your readers. Do you have a will? Mom – Mom had cashed in her insurance somewhere along the line. Probably for someone's education. Maybe mine. But she had no will and she had no insurance. She did have debt. Anyway, that's something for people to check into. Early.

Mom went into the hospital. And never came back. She went to the Convalescent and Rehabilitation Center in Winona, Minnesota. They were incredible. Awesome. The doctor told her she had six months to live, but she lived for two-and-a-half years.

Mom loved it there. She had always had service jobs, and here she was queen. Everyone was waiting on her. And, for all the things about small towns – the things that aren't great – one thing, in a crisis, they're always there. They were really wonderful. Everyone was going from my town to Winona to visit with her. People liked to talk with my mom. And my stepdad – he turned into a real king. He took very good care of her then. I don't know what it was, but he was very good to her.

We came every month by train. Sometimes, we'd plop the kids in the car and drop them off at my husband's parents'. And then have some time for just us. We actually had some nice weekends going to

Winona. We didn't spend all the time at the hospital. I saw old high school friends. We enjoyed being outside in that area. We just really relaxed and had fun.

I did find out you have to kind of fight for your rights with these things. Mom said to me, "I wonder if I'm getting better – or else they're leaving me here to rot."

Mom's mind was very astute. She stayed like that until the end. So I checked into it and found out a doctor visit was overdue. Medicare demands that the doctor visit on a certain schedule.

This was Mom's old family doctor, who golfed with my stepdad, knew them well. Al didn't want me to interfere.

He said, "Of course, he's doing his job!"

I called the doctor about it, anyway. He was right there to see Mom. But it caused a rift with Al that never healed. He thought I was interfering.

One thing about it all that was really fun – my kids were little at the time. And we moved to Fargo toward the end, which was just about six hours away. So, I'd take one kid at a time. It was really neat to have time alone with them, just like with my husband. It was one thing that wasn't sad about it all.

For about two years, we went once a month. Then – she just slept away. I remember her last words to me were, "I'm really pooped! You can go now."

She was just so tired.

I didn't need to do the death watch. My brother was there. He came and he sat with her. He and Al. Al was still hanging in. I think if I'd lived closer, I would have had it worse. But she had many, many friends. I could walk away knowing that it was that kind of community. The kind that would take care of her. I knew she was getting wonderful care.

After Mom died, we continued seeing Al. Mostly for humanitarian reasons. Not for love. He had no family, no one else. He had always been gruff, but he was getting worse. He lived about eight years after mother died, and he just kept getting harder to be with. We went at Christmas and a few times during the year.

It was hard to see that he was getting ill, but he was. Some friends had moved him into a senior citizen's center – full of grumpy old men! Al was abrasive, resentful, I think, about what life had done to him.

Pretty soon, it was just me going. The rest of the family just bagged it! It was really icky there. I'd just sit on the couch and grade papers while he watched TV. Then he'd go to bed.

He had a friend that took him to the doctor. He had a liver thing, and then his kidneys started to go. He had to get the fluid tapped. He'd just fill up. And Al was so mean to the man. I don't know why he even kept taking him.

I was teaching more at this point and the kids were all in school. In the summer they'd go once. He was so mean-spirited, you kind of felt bad for this guy. The thing was, I didn't like the kids around him. He talked – well, he was always using racial slurs and things I just didn't want the kids to be listening to. So the kids' trips got fewer and fewer.

My brother came occasionally. It was a long trip for him, and he'd been treated the worst by Al, since he'd actually lived with him when he was a kid. My brother did his paperwork. Whoever was there got all the grief. Whoever was not there was the good one.

Again, I relied heavily on this little community. I couldn't be there a lot, and I didn't feel guilty, because Al was so difficult.

Then he finally died, and I was – relieved.

Al was good to my mom at the end, but he was a miserable man. I hope now he's in a better place. He's buried by my mom, and my real dad is in another cemetery, so that's kind of....

You know, another thing that needs to be considered in all this. There are all these systems involved. All these people with all these needs. There were times when my husband's parents felt used. And times, like when my child cut a finger and my mother-in-law blamed me. Her reaction was, "Your child got hurt! Where were you? Why weren't you here?"

Their father was with them and so were their grandparents!

I'm just glad it's all over. It's kind of like a play – a drama with the sick person sort of center stage. And we're all playing in the drama. Some of it was very good. But, I'm glad it's over.

Chapter Twenty
Steve

Local lore has it that we have two seasons – winter and road construction. I'm traveling west on south Thirteenth Avenue, headed toward the West Acres area with Barnes and Noble my destination. I should have remembered the road construction and taken Interstate 29. Too late now.

Steve and I are going to meet for coffee on his way from Valley City, North Dakota to Minneapolis, Minnesota to visit his mother. This is an easy pit stop from Interstate 94.

We've only met once, a few months back, when he was visiting a friend of mine. I do hope I recognize him.

I drive into the lot a bit late, walk through the wooden double doors, and find my way through the wonderland of books back to the café.

Ah, there he is. Hunched over a soda reading *Sports Illustrated*. "Hey, Steve! How's the drive?"

"Carol! Have a chair. The drive's a piece of cake in the summer. The winter trips are the ones that do me in."

"Yeah, it's gorgeous out now. Just don't get tied up on Thirteenth Avenue. "So, how goes it with your mother?" I ask.

Steve is wound up and ready to pitch.

***

It's all so nuts. Just nuts. I have my job and family at home, all of which need my time. But I'm always worried about my mom. I'm the only one left to take care of things. It really keeps me stirred up.

When I was growing up, my mom was always gone. She was an entertainer, first in Bismarck, North Dakota – then we moved to

Minneapolis because of it. She had a celebrity personality. She felt naturally entitled.

Mother was always dressed up, with dramatic clothes and makeup. She was a star. We'd go out to these places and play the role. I loved it then, but now I've gone the other way, and really despise that whole lifestyle. I'm really a feet on the ground guy. But she loved the limelight, and we were always in it if we went out.

She grew up wealthy, with a take charge, do your own thing personality. She just wasn't worried about other people. Mom married four times – three after my father. The last three were alcoholics. Dad was a workaholic. He died in '78. I was really angry when he died because he never gave me what I needed – which I now know was love. But that was how I felt.

Now that I've grown and gotten more education, I realize he did the best he could. I've worked it through and the good times came back, so now I think of him with a lot of love.

Mom took care of her last husband for four years when he was sick before he died. I despised the guy, but she stuck with him until the end. Then when he died, she changed. She got back in touch with me after all those years of coolness.

She was always the rugged individualist, but when her last husband died, that seemed to die too. She gave up everything then, even her crossword puzzles.

Her health deteriorated. She's had some seizures, and she's getting really fearful. She even stopped some of glamour stuff, except for dining at the country club. That she still must do. I say, "Mom, can't we go somewhere else? I'm tired of the food here."

But she still loves that atmosphere, so we go there to eat every time I visit.

She takes medication for her seizures, and can drive, but she's afraid to. I've tried to get her to at least go the grocery store, but she won't do it. She eats well, takes her medication okay. I take her grocery shopping each month when I drive down. But she could go just to get out. Maybe pick up a few things. She won't do it, though.

I can see her memory is getting pretty bad, so maybe that's why. She does okay, but I noticed when I was down there doing her taxes, she was pretty forgetful. And yet, she does her checkbook, eats well. I don't know. She has always manipulated people, and I sometimes wonder if that's what this is about. She does fine when she's alone, and then when I come, she has all these problems!

I know I have a complicated relationship with my mom. It's a love-hate thing. I can say that now. See, my wife and my mother just despise each other. Oh, my wife's getting a little better. I've stopped reacting to her negative stuff, just let it go, but it bothers me. I was there for her with her parents, but she can't do that for me.

Yet, in a way, I can't blame her. My mother has pushed everyone away. Even the grandchildren. She just says such mean things. Sometimes I hate her. But she's my mother. I love her because of that. The more enmeshed I get with this, the worse it gets. It's just a hard time, that's all.

Some of it's my problem. I'm leaving on vacation and I've been nuts about it. Being gone in case she needs me – so I called her today and I said, "Say, Mom, will you be okay when I'm on vacation?"

She said, "I'm fine."

Now, after hearing that, *I'm* fine. My God!

Mom is still in her house and that's another worry. She wants to stay there, but she complains about the problems, the yard, the repairs. I say, "Mom, you should think about a condo or an apartment. You've got plenty of money. You can move and then we'll sell your house. I'll do it all."

But she's an oppositional person. You bring it up and she doesn't want it.

Finally she agreed to a move. My first thought is, I want her close. But how close? She calls me every day! My wife hates her! How close do I want her to live?

I know it really would be easier, logistically, to have her closer, though. So I found a great place in town, just a beautiful place. I arranged to get it. It had assisted living and that was good. She said okay. Then she changed her mind. She didn't want to move in the winter. So I had to let it go.

We went through that twice more. I worry. Will there be an opening when she needs it? Will it offer enough care? If she waits too long she'll need more care. Will she need a nursing home?

Then I get worried about the money. She has plenty of money, but it could all go for the nursing home. Then I feel really awful because I even thought about the money and the fact that her care will use it all up. I've pretty well worked that through, but it's given me some guilt.

I'm checking out nursing homes in the area, and hope to find one that's really good. I want her to be happy. Of course, I know my mom, and she won't be happy anywhere. Only an act of God – and I realize that is possible – but only an act of God could make her get down to the level of other people and have friends and be happy. I know I can't do that for her.

I wonder all the time, am I doing enough? Then I tell myself, "My God, you're only one person!" I'm very busy with my own family. I get pulled in all directions. I remind myself that it's my choice where I put my time.

But it really isn't. I'm locked in by values. This is the path I've chosen for now. For this day. I will just have to set limits. Somehow, someway. I hope I do it.

I've always had a problem dealing with death, too, and I've been denying that she will die before I do and then I'll have to deal with that. Yeah, I was acting like it just wouldn't happen. Now I'm working with it, trying to learn to deal with the concept. But I don't want to lose my mom.

It's all these questions! I've had to check around with other people who have older parents. Like, why do I have to be the parent? It doesn't feel right. People need to know what other people are doing. Am I doing this right?

I know I'm more aware than I used to be. About life itself. I look at life as a total circle. I have to learn all that I need to learn before I leave this world. And this is part of it. I'm a hard learner, but I know you only have the tools you have and most of us do the best with what we've got. I can forgive – that much I've learned. But I still have questions.

Chapter Twenty-One
Nancy

Back in the days when my boys and I camped in the children's room of the Fargo Public Library, Nancy worked behind the checkout desk. She then took a leap and became the bookmobile librarian, which means that she has maneuvered that mighty whale of a vehicle through city streets and around neighborhood parks for many years. Mind you, I found my 1968 Volkswagen roomy. And difficult to park. So I'm impressed.

Nancy hears me as I open the heavy utility door, and comes out of a room on her left. Red cotton jacket, black pants, neat brown hair and patient smile; still the Nancy I remember from the children's room. Her office is tucked behind the holding tank, er – garage, where she keeps the bookmobile, and I remark on the convenient location.

Wood paneling and furniture warm the utilitarian room, and I forget the sleeping creature just beyond the wall. Until, that is, midway through our conversation, I hear a fearsome roar, my chair trembles, a loud rumble shakes the room.

Nancy cheerfully assures me that someone is seeing to its needs, and continues with her story as if this were a normal setting.

***

I'm right smack in the middle of seven kids. We've always been a close-knit family, so when my dad went into heart surgery one afternoon and suddenly died, it was very hard on all of us. Mom was just 64, and it was hardest on her.

My brother also died – he was just 44 – so that was another blow. So we all try to help her out as much as we can.

We kind of have the understanding that my youngest sister helps clean and takes mom for groceries and things. She has a daycare and it would affect too many people for her to take Mom to her doctor appointments, so I'm the one who does that. We go for something about every other week. She doesn't drive – she still has her license and her car, but she's not comfortable driving much and we don't want her to do it. There's pretty much always someone to drive her.

Her memory is good – better than mine! She has arthritis. She has had a hip replacement, and then she went in for knee surgery, but she didn't pass the physical. They decided to do a triple bypass. They're still working on her knee – giving her some injections to lubricate the joint and help the pain until her health improves enough for surgery. She also has Crohn's disease, which causes cramping and diarrhea.

This last six months has been bad. She has some allergy they can't figure out. She gets hives – big welts that swell – and twice, her tongue has swollen so large it nearly choked her. She has a shot kit to use, but because of the side effects they don't want her to use it unless she has to. They'd rather she go to emergency. They think the hives are from stress or something, since they can't figure anything else out.

It's been one thing after the other these last weeks. I have two brothers here in town. They're wonderful, but, well, they're men. For the doctor appointments, it works better with a daughter.

My job here – they're wonderful. I work with two ladies. Older ladies – put that in! I always tease them. They're very understanding about this, about my taking Mom to the doctor.

I work full time in four days – sometimes 12-hour days – but that gives me Friday off. So, naturally we try to go on Fridays. But we can't always do it then, so they give me lots of support.

I have to tell you, I have the best family in the world. They are always there for Mom – and for me. I have a brother and sister, both who live in Fort Collins, Colorado. They came and stayed with her when she had her hip surgery. Though it's easy for me to take time off when I need to, ten days is too much.

I think after losing my brother – well, I'm not sure that's something a mother ever gets over. I think that after that, she's been even more nervous about her heart, too. My dad, my brother, her siblings – all had heart problems.

She's getting to the point where she's really worried about living alone. There are a lot of us around. Someone visits nearly every evening, but she's still alone at night, and nights are always hard when you have a lot of pain. And a lot of worry. You know how the mind works. So she has trouble sleeping.

We've looked into getting a roommate. She's just so active and alert, she's not ready for a nursing home. But – well – a roommate, after all these years! You never know who you'll get.

She says, "I'm kind of set in my ways, and how do you know about people?"

I know there's a lot of loneliness in the evenings.

Just the thought of something happening, and no one being there. We really do have to decide what to do.

She was a good mom and a good grandma. We're so fortunate to have so many of us. It's a real blessing, though, I don't know if Mom thought so when we were young!

I know she depends on us a lot. My oldest brother helps her with her finances and questions like about insurance and things. She still does her own checkbook, though.

Mom has a friend who picks her up and they go swimming at the "Y" twice a week. She loves that. She was always scared to death of the water, but this isn't deep and it's warm. She says it's like she has no pain when she's in the water.

My mother never has been one who liked to take medicine, so it's been a real challenge to get her to take it. Though with the Crohn's disease – well, the pain was so bad the other night that she nearly called 911. It's so hard to even do things with her friends, because you never know how it's going to be. You don't dare get away from a bathroom. And the stomach pain is horrible. She's had so many tests, but you just don't get anywhere.

Mom says she can live with the knee, but the stomachache – it's horrible. She experiments with food, but it has almost nothing to do with what she eats.

These last few years – since Dad's been gone – she hates cooking for herself, so I know she doesn't eat well when she's alone. About four times a week, my sister cooks extra and takes it over. We all go over for supper a lot, because Mom still loves to cook for us.

My husband is very supportive. He's always understanding when I need to be gone. His mother is widowed. He's an excellent son and does a lot of things around her house for her, so that's never a problem for me.

To me, it's very natural to help. I mean, Mother was always there when we needed her. I don't think this is a hardship on me – I think it was planned from the beginning. Maybe because there are so many of us to do things, it's easier for us than it would be otherwise. My whole family has a wonderful sense of humor. Laughter is good for the soul, I guess. Sometimes, that's how you get through the day.

It's what life's all about. I hope my children are there for me when I grow old. You know, I watched my mother. She was there for her parents. Grandma died of cancer. Then Mother took care of my grandpa – did his laundry, made sure he ate. It's just how it all works.

Alice Warne Bursack

Chapter Twenty-Two
Alice In Wonderland

I drove into the approach by the condo garages, and parked in my mother-in-law's space, popped the trunk, and grabbed the bag with my curling brush and spray conditioner. Bottles of apricot juice and boxes of date pocket cookies had been frolicking in my trunk since I first turned right on Broadway. I collected the scattered items and wrestled the bags from the trunk. Alice's keys bit my palm under the handles of two bags.

I toted the other two bags in my left hand with my purse. I'd brought deli stew and some hot vegetable soup, hoping one of them would appeal to her, but it was the cookies and juice she usually wanted.

When I set down the two bags in my right hand so I could open the door, the keys slipped into a bag. While I dug for the keys, a bottle of apricot juice slid onto the ice. I picked up the juice before it tumbled down the cement steps, tried again to hook the keys, replaced the juice, and opened the door. I clank, clanked the bags, two per hand, up the long single flight of green carpeted steps, to Alice's door.

Knocking once, I opened the door. "Hi! It's me!" I hollered. Like she was expecting Mr. Rogers. Alice sat among her papers on the couch, shrouded in the surreal light filtering through closed sea green curtains. Even her icy white hair, standing out from her head like porcupine quills, had taken on the eerie glow. She was writing her name, over and over and over on a yellow legal pad. Alice, Alice, Alice.

"I brought you lunch," I said, as I said every day. "And I brought my curling brush. I'm your new hairstylist."

She oriented herself as she watched me unload bags in the kitchen, and pour some hot soup in a bowl.

"Okay if I open your drapes?" I asked.

"That would be nice," she said.

She smiled at me and pulled herself up from the couch, then navigated her walker around the furniture toward the kitchen table.

While Alice picked at her soup, pushing the vegetables around like toadstools in grass, I took a stab at tidying up the kitchen and set up the hair supplies.

"Did you have all you want?" I asked her, not wanting to prolong her discomfort. "We can always heat something else later."

"That was really good," she said.

"Great," I answered, as I moved the virtually full soup bowl aside. "Let's make you gorgeous."

She laughed as I started twisting her hair around the heated brush. I had no business inflicting my lack of skill on another person, but she was afraid to sit in the rail chair to go down the steps, so I couldn't get her to a beautician anymore.

"Oooo, I'm sorry. I've really got it stuck," I said.

The brush dangled from a mat of hair. I jiggled it and pulled it, wondering if Alice would notice a bald spot on the back of her head. She needed a perm. She needed a beautician. She needed somebody with some skill.

"I'm sure it will be fine," she said, with only slight nervousness. "But I think you're almost done."

"Almost," I told her, as I freed the brush. "But maybe we should try to get both sides curled, instead only one. Just for fun."

"I'm sure it will be fine," she said again.

I took that to mean that she hoped she'd still have some hair left when I finished. Finally, I achieved a bit of symmetry and called it a hairdo.

Loneliness had caused Alice to perceive anything other than her close surroundings as a threat. Anything past her door. The newspaper which lies on the carpet just outside. The cars driving by. The ring of the phone.

Food grew in her refrigerator. Mail and magazines multiplied on her couch, chairs and tables. She didn't like the home care people who came to bathe her or the nurse who came to take care of her feet. Her children had already decided that she needed to move across the avenue to Rosewood, and Rosewood had put her on their waiting list.

We were surprised when, after being told a room was available, Alice accepted the news with calm. She allowed us to put her in the rail chair, motor her down, help her into the car, and drive her across the avenue to Rosewood's sheltered entrance.

Alice pushed her walker through the vestibule and into the lobby as though she were going to visit a friend. She wasn't interested in looking out the window, across the avenue, to see her condo. She wasn't interested in looking out the sunroom window to see Broadway. She made a clean break.

"Hi, Alice," Lynette, at the reception desk, said.

"Well, Alice, welcome!" Teri, in admissions, said.

"Come on Gram," I told Alice. "Let's go up to third floor. Your room is on the same floor as Dad's."

Alice nodded, looked around briefly, and said, "I used to come here."

"That's right," I said. "When your church circle came to meet each year with Leone. Now, they'll come and hold a meeting here with you." Alice seemed pleased knowing that her circle meetings would once again be a part of her life.

She hesitated only slightly at the elevator, then we got on and rode to third floor. Lynn was to be Alice's aide. Beautiful blonde Lynn took Alice by the arm and ushered her to her room.

"She's all mine, now," Lynn said.

She winked at Alice. Alice giggled. I was grateful. She seemed to be doing well.

"I'll run over to your...uh...the condo, and get your clothes," I said.

Alice nodded and let Lynn fuss over her. I moved in some clothes and personal things, and promised to bring more when I visited tomorrow.

Alice stayed happy. Her cheeks pinked up, her hair, regularly set (by a professional) was again an airy white dandelion puff. She pushed her walker around Rosewood, attending chapel, pie day, Bible study, live music, and, when all else failed, bingo.

"Alice is so sweet," said an aide.

"She's always smiling," said another.

"Alice is so nice," said still another.

"She's playing the piano!"

"She entertains us with the organ. Did she really play the church organ?"

"Oh, she was a very gifted musician," I answered.

"I hear Alice taught school."

"And her needlework. She has such beautiful needlework in her room."

Alice's life at Rosewood gave her a social transfusion. She enjoyed being Alice once more. It lasted until her first bout with pneumonia, and then the juices started to drain. Now, several years later, she's drying up. The old paranoia is returning and with only a sliver of memory remaining, confusion is her next of kin. She's tired. She's weak. She's had enough.

Alice was an intelligent, accomplished mother of four. She has lived a gentle life, and, now, in her nineties, she deserves a gentle death. I pray that Alice will one night slip away as kindly and quietly as she lived.

Chapter Twenty-Three
Michelle

I find a parking place right in front of Cynthia's Custom Cakes. Her moss green sidewalk tables sit empty this chilly morning. They'll soon go into hibernation for the winter.

Inside, the homey fragrance of maple syrup calls me toward the antique pastry counter, but I snub it and take a table near the front window. A group of women, immersed in chatter, drink coffee and eat bagels at a table in the rear.

I savor the aura created by the century-old wood, pressed-tin ceiling, antique framed pictures and yummy smells, then scribble a few notes on my pad. A tall, slim woman with loose chestnut hair and olive skin pushes through the door and looks around the room. I smile at her, and she walks over.

"Michelle?"

"You must be Carol."

Michelle and I get acquainted as we wait by the counter. I bond with the cheesecake, but Michelle gracefully declines, so I pass on the goodies. By the time we carry our house coffee to the table, we've cranked up a good conversation, and Michelle has already begun telling her story.

***

I was the baby of three kids, and my sister and I, especially, grew up very close. She's my saint. I don't know what I would have done without her.

In just one year, my whole life just kind of fell apart. It began when my pre-teen son, Chad, began having terrible problems. We went through all the counseling in school, then with social services and psychologists. He was eventually diagnosed with bi-polar disease, but they haven't been able to manage it well, so the stress and pain have been with us ever since.

The same year Chad's problems started, my mother was diagnosed with lung cancer. Chad was very close to my mom and my stepdad, so this added to his problems.

Just before her surgery, Mom – a long-time smoker – said, "I've had my last cigarette." And it was. After her surgery, she was okay – but not totally okay – for the next couple of years. She never really got healthy. One thing – we were lucky in that way – that Mom got worse gradually.

She didn't really get bad until the last week before she died. The cancer went from her lung to her bones and then – it was on Mother's Day – she found out it was in her brain. That's when she said she didn't want any more treatment. She just quit it all. She still looked so good, though! I thought, "How can you look so good when you are dying?"

We brought in hospice that last week, but she died within a few days. We were so glad that she didn't have to be dragging out in pain, lingering for months and months like you think of cancer patients.

What I have the hardest time with is that – the last day, she was trying to tell me something – she never got it out. She couldn't speak, but she was trying so hard. I still wonder....

Chad was still having terrible problems during this time. He'd be in a horrible depression, or else so manic he was uncontrollable. Eventually, he just left home. We were always there for him, but it was awful never to know where he was. And it was awful when he was home, too.

And then my Aunt Sheila – she'd lived with us for years when I was a kid – it became obvious that she wasn't well. She was getting pretty mixed up, and really strange about money. She was always so worried she would run out. She'd sit in the dark, and she wouldn't eat because it cost money. Once she put a kettle on the stove, and it started smoking when she forgot about it. Someone called 911. She said the next time she put something on the stove, she would shove a rug against the door, so no one would report it!

We knew she needed care, so we moved her into the Fairmont. Once she got into the retirement home she started gaining weight, because she started eating. Actually, she just continued to gain until she was a very big woman at her death!

Sheila was at the Fairmont for several years, but then, one day she ended up on the floor, and they decided she needed to go into the hospital. It was funny, she was so cranky there. She said to me, "Get me some cigarettes." She was dying to smoke.

I was mainly in charge of her care. She had a family in Wisconsin, but they weren't able to come out much. They did come out to see her before she died. But they had health problems of their own, so with the hospital's help, I had to decide the nursing home question and she went to Bethany. I'd been doing all her paperwork, her Medicaid and things.

During this time, also, my husband's father began to get really hard to control. I don't know if it was Alzheimer's or what – but he was impossible. And my mother-in-law – I love her dearly – but she would have preferred to take care of Oscar herself. After all, she had taken care of him at home for four years, this little woman and this big man. But she finally agreed to put him in a nursing home. She made darned sure the staff at Bethany was doing everything right for Oscar!

Eventually he went into the hospital and he would have died except she made them put in feeding tubes. We were all very distressed. My husband is very open about these things, and he didn't want that. But once the tubes are in – well, there's nothing you can do about it. Luckily, he passed away in a fairly short time anyway. It was such a relief. Just like when my mother died. They don't have to just lie there.

Then Sheila got sick. She was sick about a month, though she was only in distress for a few days. Bethany was really good about following advance directives. I had signed papers for her to have whatever she needed for comfort but no life prolonging measures. She had oxygen, and I authorized pain medication and antibiotics. She couldn't fight off her illness, but was good until nearly the end. No horrible suffering.

My stepdad had retired the year before my mother got sick. He'd been a busy lawyer, and found himself without a wife or a job. He was an alcoholic who never could stand being alone, and after Mom died, he really took a dive. It was bad. Then he ran into this woman he had known in the past. She has five grown kids who never really paid any attention to her.

After they got married, our family moved her into his house. Then Dad had her house fixed up and they sold it. She was a drinker, too, and a real hell-raiser. She had a lot of brain damage from drinking and probably already had Alzheimer's.

We babysat the two of them back and forth. She didn't eat and didn't want him to eat either. Dad got sick and ended up in the hospital. His liver was shot and he was in bad shape in all ways. Believe it or not, they weaned him off booze. He rallied and went home. Then, he spent the last six weeks of his life going through his things, sorting and throwing much of it away. He seemed driven to get through it all.

He kept getting sicker. He didn't want to go to a home, so we got him 24-hour care. But that wasn't reliable at all. We got some private people and some from an agency, but they couldn't cover all the hours. It was a mess. One young man we hired as the main cook – he wasn't from the agency, but he seemed so nice – he used Dad's bank card. There were other things missing too. We never could tell exactly what happened.

Meanwhile, Dad's wife continued to harass the caregivers and sabotage their efforts to care for him. She began taking his medicine, and all kinds of weird combinations of medicines and things she wanted us to get when we got groceries. She couldn't drink because we didn't get booze, but she was taking whatever drugs she could.

We had hospice come in for Dad, and his wife was terrible to them. She kept hiding their supplies, and was totally belligerent. For example, she would have a tantrum when they tried to change Dad's bedding. Finally we bought new sheets for his bed, but she still had a fit.

I remember Dad called me once – one awful day, when I'd been over there all day and was all stressed out – I'd even had a minor car accident on the way over. He called me and wanted me to come back. He wanted to tell me something. It was seven o'clock at night – I'd been over there all day.

I said, "Can you tell me on the phone?"

It seemed like it was about food, but he couldn't get it out. I wondered all night if I should have gone back. Of course, the next day when I went, he couldn't remember what it was. But... that will haunt me in my grave. I should have gone over there... but... I'd just left....

The night he died – we had just left when it happened. We went back. And when they were carrying his body out of the house, his wife kept fussing that they might damage something. I don't think she was thinking of his death at all.

When he died we found out that she had talked him into leaving her his house, our little farmstead, and all his money. It's kind of heartbreaking, now, to drive by that house. She's dead, and her kids have let it get all run down. That's where I grew up. My mom died there. My stepdad died there.

The channel running through all of this was my son's problems. And then my own health. I've been diagnosed with clinical depression. It has all taken its toll.

I still wonder if I made the right decisions. When you're young, you don't think that you're going to grow old and die. You just don't realize all of this. If I knew I was going to die – as Mom knew – would I do anything different? If I knew that today was my last day on earth, how would I live?

Chapter Twenty-Four
Karen

I was at a Straus picnic. Well - actually a Rob picnic, since it was at his house. It's sort of complicated, but our host, Rob, was sending wonderful whiffs of roast beef from his grill, as dishes of salads and desserts were piling up on long tables crammed with chattering guests. Straus Clothing has been a family-owned pillar of eastern North Dakota for well over a century, and friends and employees need little excuse to gather. I qualified for entrance.

Karen and I are responding well to the call of good food. The evening is cool, just 60 degrees, and it feels good. When people meet me they immediately start talking about old people (?), so Karen and I begin a conversation that drifts to her Aunt Florence, their aging family matriarch.

I say, "Hold that story!"

We make an appointment to meet in her office at a local hospital, where she works as the director of nursing, so I can get it down on paper.

Karen ushers me into her large, open, newly decorated office. She's tall and impressive in a black suit and embroidered, creamy silk blouse. I'm feeling a bit Liliputian and am grateful she doesn't offer me a phone book to place in my chair as a booster, though it would, indeed, give me more presence. I whip out my notepad as Karen tells her story.

***

The thing about Florence was that she was always a spitfire. In fact when Florence told me stories about when she was younger, she always said she was a snot. She had dedicated her early life to taking care of her younger siblings. What she meant by her being a snot is, she was so protective that she'd do things like when she walked her kid brothers to school and they got there cold, she'd push the other kids away from the pot bellied stove so her siblings could get warm.

She remained very focused on family all of her life. Although she did marry, she never had children of her own. She spent her days – well, depending on whose version you listen to – my mother's was that she spent her days interfering in other people's child rearing. But if you were talking to one of us kids – she spent her days making our lives special. She was our Santa Claus. She always gave to us – herself, as well as gifts.

Aunt Florencie – we all called her Aunt Florencie – demanded a certain kind of behavior from us kids in return. Kindness, doing as we were asked, and especially loyalty to family. She brought make believe to life. Everything had to be special. Nothing was routine for her. Every holiday was celebrated. It brought her a sense of satisfaction to give.

Florence comes from the generation of women who took care of their men. The men came in from the fields and were fed huge meals. They were taken care of in all ways around the house. After she left the farm, she became a city girl. But she still kept the idea of a sort of caste system in the family. First the men, then the children, then the women.

We drifted apart some when I finished college because I moved east to Washington, D.C., and I didn't see that much of her. But I woke up one day and I thought, "What is life about, anyway?" I guess you can't take the Midwest out of the person. I knew I had to move back home. I was very specialized in my field, and East Grand Forks, Minnesota where my family lived, couldn't offer the right kind of position, but I found what I wanted in Fargo right away.

While I was out east, Florence had moved to Minneapolis to take care of an older sister. During that time, Florence's husband died and the sister had a stroke. She brought her sister back to East Grand Forks where she felt better able to care for her. Florence still had that sparkle of life. That caring. I saw the dedication she gave to her older sister, Ethel, while Ethel lived out her final days in the nursing home.

How she changed the room decorations to match all the holidays. How she did everything she could to make things special for her. Then Ethel died.

Florence had begun to develop some behavior problems herself – like strange ways of labeling and filing things in envelopes. Just different traits that would develop over time. Then she started having mini-strokes.

The big turning point – where she needed someone to help her – was during the flood in '97. Florence and her sister-in-law, Helma, were evacuated by Helma's son David, with barely a suitcase. The flood pushed them out of town, and they had no time to save Florence's things, which were stored in the basement. Dave whisked them off to Grafton, North Dakota to live with him, and they were there about ten months. So, everything that would have helped Florence remember – hang on to her past – was gone. All of her personal belongings – her keepsakes, her scrapbooks, her snapshots, her history – it was all lost.

She was placed in a new environment in Grafton. When they finally got the house restored enough to get back into it, she was like a nomad roaming the desert. Her things were all still gone.

She and Helma continued to live in the house together, but Florence began getting worse. She was getting up at night, shining a light in Helma's face, listening to voices she thought she heard. Helma was frightened and the relationship wasn't going well. I think Helma realized she was slipping too, and that was frightening for her. There would be fights and on a couple of occasions, Florence even lifted her hand.

It broke Helma's heart the day she had to call me and say, "Karen, you have to help me."

I was the oldest female of the next generation in the family, my kids were gone from home and I hadn't been burned out yet. And didn't Aunt Florencie deserve what she'd given all her life? Attention, devotion and love.

So Aunt Florencie came to live with us in Fargo, on Valentines Day of '98. My husband was fantastic. So tolerant of Florencie's repeated questions and her – habits. I could never have done it without him. She fussed over our dog and slipped him food all the time. He became her great friend.

I really had to change my lifestyle. I was casually dropping in at lunchtime, to be sure she ate and took her pills. It was hard to care for someone who was so unwilling to accept care. This is when the role reversal came. I didn't know how to talk sternly or to be firm with Aunt Florencie. I didn't know how to get her to do what she needed to do. Oh, there were times when she was lucid, but....

One of the things that was the toughest – you almost give them too much credit for what they're doing and deciding – because she was so good at camouflaging, she could cover up her problems very well. It really became clear, however, how bad she was getting when we took her along in the motorhome to the lake. It was sensory overload. She started hallucinating again – she became a raving maniac. She was paranoid. She was angry. She'd point her finger at us and say, "Don't you think you're fooling me!"

Then she'd go into this bizarre scene....

I called a nurse hotline back home and they were great. They said, "Well, we'll give her a workup and see what's going on."

So back home we went. She was diagnosed with senile dementia with hallucinations. Of course, to this day, she knows that her head would be better if I'd get her new glasses! We had everything checked, just to be sure, but that was the diagnosis.

I was very concerned that she not come back to the house. It would be such a fight to get her into a nursing home then. Really, it would hurt that much more – I mean, all of us. But I knew it had to be done. So seven or eight months after coming to live with us, Florencie went to Villa Maria. I thought, great, they have child care and pets running around that nursing home. She'll be busy taking care of them all. But it didn't work that way. She worried too much about whether or not they were being taken care of. It upset her so much she just couldn't be involved.

This was a woman with no hobbies! She just sat and fussed. Her confusion scared her. "How will I ever get a ride? Where am I supposed to be?"

When I visited, I tried to redirect her by talking about her favorite nurse, or something. But, she would get off in other areas.

She had a lot of personal things around her by then, some things like a special lamp that had been upstairs in the house in East Grand Forks. But what she continues to fuss about to this day is – the shades of her nylons! The black must be worn with black, the blue with blue.

Because she had no hobbies, she was and is very dependent on family to visit and to be her life. She'll tear your heart strings. When she was more lucid, she'd whisper, almost childlike, "Just put me in your suitcase and take me with you!"

I have to tell her yes and no for things, and I'm still not used to that. This year is the first time I've ever seen her cry for herself. She said, "Is there any quality to my life? It's always been the family, the family, the family. Why can't I live with you? I won't bother you."

Because, to her, life is family. Without family, she has no life.

The other nieces and nephews and all of us feel a real sense of providing some quality of life to her, because she was so giving in her lifetime. But we can't really give up our jobs. Sometimes, I think, even if we had to go on welfare – that's what we should do!

This aging process has been driven home more for me by this. We try to make light of it, but it's caused me to stop and think. I make jokes about my computer chip being full when I forget something. We're aware – I guess it's do unto others as you would have them do....

I wonder who will help us when we reach those troubled days?

Chapter Twenty-Five
David

I hadn't talked to David for thirty years. We met a few times when his girlfriend, Samantha, now his wife, was a cohort of mine while we worked in Europe in the late sixties. Sam and I have corresponded ever since, and can pick up our conversation anytime, mid-sentence, and barrel along as if we never parted.

Writing this book reminded me of Sam's parents, who live on the east coast. She'd told me they were in declining health, and I called her to ask how they were doing. She spoke of her worries, and how glad she was that her sister lived near them, because they would soon be needing help.

She then told me about David's father's death. The logistics of San Francisco to Florida caregiving fueled my curiosity, so Sam volunteered her husband as a storyteller. David and I made a date.

I call at the appointed moment and the strong, confident voice of a California businessman answers. The brisk businessman's voice gradually softens to that of a proud son as David tells his story.

***

My mom died a number of years ago, but my dad had just kept going strong. He'd always been in outstanding health. I mean really outstanding. He almost never got sick.

When he was out to see us Christmas of 1996, we noticed he'd lost a little weight. We asked him how he felt and he said, "Now don't get upset, but I'm going in for a gallbladder operation in a couple of weeks."

We really weren't too worried. He was just so healthy. The operation was to be in January. A couple of weeks after he left us, I was here in the office. I got a call from one of his neighbors. He said dad had gone to the bathroom, and he found a lot of blood in the toilet, so he called an ambulance and they took him in to the hospital.

I thanked my neighbor profusely, and called the hospital. They had the doctor call me back. He said they had done exploratory surgery, and that dad was full of cancer. They had to put off the gallbladder surgery, and take care of the cancer first.

I sat there thinking to myself, "Well, that's just one opinion." I called Dad's normal doctor – the one he'd been seeing for years. He told me that dad had lymphoma.

I said, "What are his chances?"

He said that actually the prognosis was pretty good.

I called Dad, and was able to talk to him the next day. I made arrangements to fly down to Florida, and the hospital made arrangements to send Dad home with a full-time nurse for awhile. I was so impressed with the care he got when I went down there. They had a physical therapist coming in – they'd taken care of it all.

After I got there and was talking to Dad – I'll never forget this – he said, "Well, Dave, I guess I've got a touch of cancer."

One thing you have to know about my dad. He had the most positive attitude of anyone I know. I talked with his physicians and they said, "Look, your dad's in great spirits and he's had wonderful health. We want to get a little more weight on him, and then we'll start chemotherapy."

I was wondering what I should do about care for Dad. Should I keep him at home or put him in some level of facility? What level?

I talked to the physical therapist and his doctor and they all said, "Look, your dad loves his house. And he can still get around using his walker. If anything more happens, you can always move him into the next level of care then. But let him stay home as long as he can."

Dad had always loved his yard, too. I remember when I was growing up – he'd come home from work and walk the yard before he even came in the house. When I get home – I just go in the door! But he always had to walk his yard. I decided that he needed to stay with that as long as he could.

So I got busy and started setting up a support system at home. I told them, "Look, I'll stay as long as it takes. I want him to have all the care he needs.

One of the things I did was get meals set up. The hospital had said there's a nursing service you can get and they can take care of that, too. So, I met with them and met with the lady who'd do the daily care for my dad, and they were a fit. She would come about eleven o'clock in the morning. Dad could get himself up and have some cereal and get dressed, then she came about eleven and stayed until six. She fixed his meals, did his laundry, shopping, that kind of thing.

I also got a Lifeline for him to wear around his neck. And – this is kind of interesting – Dad was getting kind of hard of hearing, and you could get this phone-lamp setup. The lamp would flash when the phone rang. The state of Florida had those available, so I went down one day and signed for one of those. I also got him a phone with big numbers for his bedroom, and programmed in all the relatives and neighbors for him.

Also, he was having a little trouble getting up from a chair, so I found one of those chairs where you just push a button and it lifts them up. I also did a kind of inventory around the house, and replaced things I thought he'd need.

We went back to see the oncologist that week.

He said, "This may sound strange, but if he has to have cancer, this is the kind for him to have. The cure rate is 70 to 80 percent. I think he'll be okay. We'll start chemo in three or four weeks."

One of the neighbors said – I just can't be emphatic enough about is this – his neighbors were unbelievable. They were really key to this whole thing. One neighbor said, "Dave, I'll drive your dad to his treatments. It's something I want to do."

Another one said, "I ride my bike every afternoon. I want you to know I'll stop in and see your dad each day, and keep an eye on him. I'll make it part of my ride."

I was there about a week and a half setting everything up. It was all covered.

I said, "Dad, I'll stay as long as I'm needed, but I think you're pretty well set up here. I'm thinking of flying back."

He told me, "Dave, I'm doing just fine now. I want to stay here. Everything is working. And what I'd really like to do is meet you and Sam and take a ride up the St. Lawrence Seaway."

I said, "Dad, you're going to lick this thing, and that's what we'll do."

I felt comfortable enough to fly back. I called all the time from San Francisco, and things were going great. His neighbor took him in for the first treatment. He did unbelievably well. A week later, he was out in his yard pulling weeds.

Then he went in for his second treatment. There was no reason for anyone to think that he wouldn't pull through just as well. But after the treatment, the same neighbor who called last time called again.

He said, "Dave, your dad's in the ICU. You'd better get back here as soon as you can."

I called dad's doctor and said, "Holy Moses! What happened?"

The doctor said, "Dave, the good part is that your dad's had good health. The bad part is that he's 85. He just couldn't take the chemo."

Well, to make a long story short, two days later I was on a plane. It was Easter morning, as a matter of fact. I went and sat with Dad. Just sat and held his hand.

Then the oncologist took me out of the room and said, "You can keep your father going – but it will be purely mechanical. Or move him out of this room. Just keep him comfortable and he'll be gone in a couple of days."

I called my sister in New York. We've always seen eye-to-eye on all of this and had been making decisions together all of this time. We decided that keeping him alive isn't what we – or he – wanted. I stayed with dad that night until about nine o'clock. I think he knew I was there – he couldn't respond, but I do think he knew I was there.

There was really no change in his condition, so I said to the nurse, "I'll go to Dad's house, it's not far away. I'll go over and sleep and clean up, and I'll be back in the morning."

I left about nine-thirty.

About eleven o'clock the nurse called and said, "You'll want to get down here. Your dad just passed away."

I went right down. It was hard. I mean, I'd say we did everything – I mean up until the last four or five days he had a great life. When they said we could keep him alive, I instantly knew that was not an option. As it turned out, we never even had to make that decision. He passed away before anything was done.

At the funeral I told people, "I'm sad, of course, to lose him, but I'm celebrating my dad's life. He would want us to celebrate."

I'm absolutely pleased I could do what I did for my dad. To be there for him. I look at it as a gift. You know, I was always very close to my mother. If someone would have asked who I was closest to, I would have said my mother. I miss her greatly. But I've got to tell you, there's not a day that goes by that I don't miss my father. He was my role model in life.

Now, I guess, I'm no longer a part of the sandwich generation. I'm the top slice of bread. I think you appreciate life more and take a longer view of things when you get in that position. My time with my dad was a very positive experience. And those neighbors – I would hope that in the years to come, that if I have the opportunity to do it, I could be like one of those neighbors myself.

Chapter Twenty-Six
Kay

I'd put out some freshly baked SunMart cookies and coffee is ready. Kay's coming to my house because she's cleaning a house on this end of town, and it's convenient.

A deep blue car, after hesitating just a bit, parks across the street. Presumably it has a driver. I peered. Ah, yes, a woman. Might be Kay.

I know very little about Kay's life, except that it's been tough. She walks quickly, blonde curls waving, looking carefree and young as she nears my front door. Her hardships don't show in her attitude. She looks cute in sweatshirt and pants, and is carrying a bottle of water.

"Hi, Kay," I say as I open the door. A cold, stiff wind blasts me as I let her in. We quickly shut the wind and the world outside.

"Come on in and have a chair. Would you like some coffee?"

"Dreamy," she says.

She follows me to the kitchen, sets her car keys and water bottle on the kitchen table and takes the cup of coffee I offer. We go into the living room to sit. Knowing her schedule, as well as the freshness of her grief, I skip the small talk.

Kay talks about Grandma.

***

My real grandma died when I was 15. I had lived with her for awhile when I was a kid, because my parents didn't want me. They were cold and abusive. Really mean to me. When my Grandma died, my parents got so tired of me crying all the time, they got me drunk. On Cold Duck.

I'm a recovering alcoholic now, Carol, and I'm very proud of it. I met Mary, the woman I soon began calling Grandma, because she lived in an apartment house managed by one of my AA friends. She needed some cleaning done, and she knew I cleaned houses, so she asked me if I'd do it. I really didn't have the time, but I said I'd do what I could.

When we met, it was instant love. I just kept going back. I cleaned for her and took home her laundry and I brought my boys to see her. She just loved the fact that I have busy boys. And the dog! I'd bring them all in.

"Just listen to that barking." She'd say.

"And those busy boys!" She'd love the chaos.

I'd try to bake once a week and bring some in to Grandma. She loved gingersnaps. I'd bring them along and we'd drink coffee, talk smart, and eat gingersnaps.

Grandma helped me work through my family history.

She knew my family wouldn't support me in recovery and she'd say, "That's their loss. We'll fix 'em. I get you all to myself. They don't deserve you!"

Grandma had lost her husband of 56 years and she said I was just what she needed. So she was needy. I was needy. Sometimes I would just go to her place to get away from all the rest of life. She was safe. I'd never had a safe place before. When I met Grandma, I think I was really hard – and cold. She helped soften me. She just gave me a different way of looking at life.

I'd come into town for my Monday and Friday morning meetings, but then I'd push the time, stay with her as long as I could. She'd shoosh me out.

She'd say, "Shoosh! Get to your meeting."

She was so proud of me – and that I was recovering. She was my spiritual advisor and helped with the rough times.

Grandma was getting so she couldn't eat anything and getting weaker, so I packed up her things and moved her to Bethany Homes. Her only family were some nieces and nephews that didn't have anything to do with her. She'd told me that they never got along, and how they'd treat her when she died.

She'd say, "They just want me to die so they can get my stuff. You mark my words, little girl, that's all they want!"

She was so feisty. God, she was a hoot! And she was right. When she moved, they came down and got the stuff they wanted. The rest went on the auction block. They took her out to dinner and left.

She'd told me she'd had cancer before, ovaries or something, when she was younger. She hadn't been eating and wasn't looking good so I said, "Grandma, you need to get to the doctor. I'll take you."

I made an appointment and when the time came, I drove into town and took her. I couldn't stay, but when I picked her up she said she was fine. Nothing wrong. He removed a cyst from her groin, and she had a rash. That was all.

But she still wasn't eating.

One day she called me up and said, "I have this horrible craving!"

It was for Rocky Road bars. So, of course, I picked some up on my way and brought them over. When I came in she said, "You're late. Two minutes late! I'm so glad to see you."

I said, "Grandma, I'm right on time. You need a new watch."

We tried the bars, but when she tried to eat, she threw up. She felt so bad.

"Oh, Honey, don't think they aren't good," she said.

I told her not to worry about it. I just wanted her to have some if they sounded good.

A week ago today she had to go into the hospital because she was so weak. She still told me she was fine. I had no idea she was so sick. They put her on an IV, and she looked so good when I saw her.

She said, "You know what's in that bag? Water and potassium! And I'll bet they're charging me a hundred bucks! It's a rip-off!"

I said, "Grandma, how long you gonna be in here?"

She said, "Four or five days."

I said, "I'll tell you what. You stay in until you are really great and when you are strong enough you come home with me for a few days."

When I went to see her Friday, she was full of energy. She was cold because she had a fever, but she was feisty.

I said, "Grandma, we're gonna have a slumber party." I curled up in bed with her and we laughed and laughed. She was just goofy that morning. She said to stop making her laugh. She'd wet her pants.

I said, "You can't, you're not wearing any!" She looked at the watch I'd brought her and said, "It's almost ten o'clock. Go! Shoosh! You'll miss your meeting."

We'd been waiting for the doctor to come in. I left and went to my meeting. When the doctor came in at 10:23, she was blue. They put her on oxygen, but when I went in on Saturday morning, she looked like she'd aged 30 years and she was in a coma.

I said, "What did you do to her? She was great yesterday!"

The doctor told me the burst of energy she'd had on Friday happens to a lot of people before they die. They said she couldn't make it through the weekend.

When I went in Sunday, she was just lying there. I sat with her and told her that now she'd get to go be with her husband.

Then I said, "Grandma, I have to go to my eleven o'clock meeting. Are you going to shoosh me?"

She moved her head – yes – and opened her eyes. When I looked back they were closed. She was dead.

You know – my real grandma and my adopted grandma would have been the same age if they both had lived. And their birthdays were on the same day. I would have liked more time with both of them.

Ruth Sandin Bradley

Chapter Twenty-Seven
Baby Ruth

Snow pellets blasted my windshield, then scattered as wiper blades scraped over an expanding film of ice. Nervous streetlights hovered over cyclones of snow. Fierce white drifts ate up the street.

It was about seven o'clock in the evening, and I'd just showered and pulled on my sweats when Lifeline called and told me Mom had set off her wrist alarm. She wasn't responding to their calls, so would I go over and check on her? I'd grown to fear the ring of the phone, which too often, meant my mom had fallen. My mom, the youngest of four children, born the year of the candy bar. Baby Ruth grown old, unable to get up from a fall.

Nausea accompanied me down Broadway, past Hornbacher's, past Hope Lutheran Church, past Trollwood Dental Offices toward Trollwood Building C, the last building on the block.

There was a parking spot close to the apartment. I parked, then leaned into my car door, pushing against the broadside wind. Dread gnawed on me. What will I find? How bad is it this time? Is she dead? Praying for strength, I got on the elevator, rode to third floor, and walked to #306.

She lay on the floor, looking chilled in a summer nightgown, the fresh daisy pattern mocking the arctic wind assaulting her window. Her left arm was twisted behind her back, her head scrunched at an angle against the wall. Blood oozed from a wound, matting her silver-fox hair; spiky red strands stuck to the white wall. Her violet-framed glasses rested a yard away next to magazines scattered like cards in a child's game. I knelt next to her and took her hand.

"Do you want me to try and move you, or should we call for

help?"

She looked at me, dazed, then rocked her head. I patted her arm and tugged down her nightgown. "I'll call the fire department," I told her. "I don't want to move you and hurt you."

As I walked to the phone, guilt edged out fear. We'd done this so often. She has two fake hips, her knees are collapsed inward, her shoulders and wrists knots of pain. She fell often.

Desperation breeds courage. I dialed 911.

"Emergency," the woman answered. Please God, let it be someone different than last week.

"My mother fell, and I'm afraid she may have broken something. I don't think we need an ambulance yet, just firefighters to see if she can be moved."

"We'll send someone out," the dispatcher answered.

I gave her the information, and sat next to Mom.

"They'll be here before long," I told her, as I rubbed her hand.

"I'll pick up the stuff so they can get through."

Bit by bit I picked up melting cubes of ice and tossed them into the sink. I moved the dismembered legs of a TV table and shoved magazines out of the path to the door. She lay silent, occasionally rocking her head.

I heard a car struggling to free itself from a snow drift. A partly deaf neighbor's TV. Water running next door. Then the rumble of men's voices, the clatter of the gurney, the rhythmic trudge of boots moving toward #306.

I opened the door to a man dressed in black pants, black boots. His black jacket, adorned with yellow reflectors, hung open, revealing red suspenders. Same as last week. Two more men in black walk up behind, each carrying a bag, one green, one orange. At least the bags had variety.

"Someone fell?" he asked.

"Yes, come in," I said.

"I was afraid to move her in case she broke something," I said, gesturing toward Mom.

Same script.

"What's her name?" he said, on cue, looking at Mom, but talking to me.

"Ruth," I said.

"Okay, Ruth. Let's see how your neck is," he said to Mom. Another man joined him and they began checking for broken bones and tended to her cut, which was, for all the blood, superficial. They asked her routine questions and declared her whole. She was now smiling sweetly at her rescuers.

"I'm fine," she said. "I just need to get up."

"I think we can do that," the first man said to her.

One man took command of her walker, while the other two took a side each, clutched under her arms and lifted her to a standing position.

"Can you stand by your walker, Ruth?" the first man asked.

"Yes, I think so," Mom answered.

"Do you think you should go to emergency, Ruth?" the man asked again.

"Oh, no, I'm fine," she answered.

"This happens a lot," I said.

"Yes, we know," he said.

I smiled charmingly.

"Uh - yes," I said.

I thanked them for coming. They clattered and thumped their way back down the hall, into the elevator, into the dark.

"Are you sure you'll be okay if I go home?" I asked.

"I'll be fine," she said.

After assuring myself repeatedly that she was okay, I helped her to the bathroom and into bed, then returned to my car and the blizzard. I plowed home.

It was nearly eleven. I'd be back at 7:30 tomorrow morning, as I was each morning, to bring her groceries, help her shower, wash clothes, unload the dishwasher, and do other chores. I'd then go home and throw in my laundry, do some of my own work, go back to get Mom and drive to Rosewood to see Dad and Alice. Then I'd take Mom home again. The days varied only in the different stops going to and from the grocery store, the drug store, the hardware store. I spun a web each day driving in and out and around an area a half-mile square.

Wednesday morning, back at Mom's, I found her still weak.

At shower time, she hesitated, nearly collapsed, and said, "I just can't do it."

"Maybe you need to go to Rosewood with Dad, so you won't be alone, at least until you get stronger," I said.

"I'm ready. I want to go," she said. "I'm scared to be alone."

My insides flopped around like a freshly landed walleye.

"I'll call Teri," I tell her.

Mom sat and had her coffee, while I phoned Rosewood, and the process began. By four o'clock we'd done everything but the required chest x-ray. The clinic would close at five. I borrowed a wheelchair from the building, wheeled Mom to the car, drove her to the clinic, had her x-rayed, and got to Rosewood by five.

We got Mom settled in her room, I went home and threw up, then spent the evening with my childhood unspooling in my brain: Mom and me burning out the mixer as we spun bright lengths of crepe paper into tight ropes to wind around milk cartons, in which all of her Cub Scouts would plant Mother's Day pansies. Mom putting League of Women Voters "VOTE" signs in our front yard. Mom as PTA president; as church deacon.

Mom in a nursing home.

Chapter Twenty-Eight
Epilogue

My three elders who were living when I wrote this book have all died.

Alice died the death I had hoped for. Not as quickly as she deserved, perhaps, but she didn't suffer terribly, either. She needed oxygen, then morphine to help her breathe. Her memory had erased nearly everything once stored. Still, she brightened when I came to visit, and the Rosewood staff said she continued to watch the elevator, knowing I would be visiting.

There were many times when it looked liked her time had come. Then she would rally a bit, and drag on. One night the phone rang, and the nurse on duty said she was, once again, showing signs of death. I hadn't gone to visit that day because I had the stomach flu. So, expecting that this was one more step along the road, I told them I was ill, but should be better by morning and I would then be up.

One of the aides, who knew Alice well, sat with her as she slept away that night. I still ache, at times, knowing that I wasn't with her at the final moment. Yet, I know that I did the right thing for everyone concerned. Alice was cared for and wouldn't have known if I were there. And I didn't make anyone else sick. It's for me that I mourn missing the moment.

Dad died in my arms. My sister is the one who suffered, having missed his moment of passing. His pain had gotten unbearable, and I kept complaining to the staff. The nurses and aides could see it in his body language, even though the doctors said, since he slept a lot, he was okay. Finally, a very spunky nurse got the message across that he needed hospice care.

From the moment Hospice of the Red River Valley took over his medications, he was comfortable. The morphine made him groggy, but he'd quit pounding his fist into his hand, grimacing as though he was trying to kill something. He was. He was trying to kill his pain. Finally, it was gone.

Dad declined quickly but peacefully. My sister and I were called one afternoon,when his decline took on more meaning. Beth drove to Fargo from Lake Park, Minnesota. Dad perked up around ten o'clock that evening. The aides turned him, washed him, and he relaxed. His color was good. Beth decided that she'd better go home, take care of the dog and drive back in the morning. I sat and held his hand, trying to decide if I should run home and try to rest a bit.

A short time later, the nurse came in to check on him, so I stepped back. She said, softly but urgently, "Carol." I moved back to the bed, cradled his head, and he died.

Such peace. For the first time in ten years I felt my dad with me. His spirit was set free from that hellish limbo and he was, once again, Dad. My son, Adam, home on the computer, felt the hug of Grandpa's spirit and knew, finally, Grandpa was well.

Beth was about halfway home. I waited to call until I was sure she wasn't driving. All I could say was what the nurse told me – "you never know." You can wait for days, go to the bathroom, and discover when you return that the person has died. Beth missed the moment, but was there through most of the process. She came to accept that this was how it happened.

Mom failed rapidly, then, as one would expect. Five months later, Beth and I sat with Mom, then under hospice care. She weighed about 85 pounds. Her legs and arms were mottled, showing signs of death, but her heart kept beating. Once again we played the guessing game – should we stay or go home and come back? I live only blocks from Rosewood, so it was easier for me. Mom was frail, but her heart was strong. Several times, over three days, we thought her heart had finally given up. We kept saying, "Go for it, Mom! Dad is waiting!" but her heart refused to free her.

One night we stayed and slept in chairs. The next night we went to our homes for a quick rest, and to shower and check on things. We waited by Mom all the next day. By early evening, I was wondering if her limbs would rot before she quit breathing. Beth and I talked of the past. We were looking at an old album with photos of our aunts – Mom's sisters, both dead – and exclaiming over each memory, when we looked up and knew. Both of us ran to her bed, held her and cheered her through the passage to the next world. Baby Ruth finally made it home.

In his lucid moments, my dad had said to me, "Do...do they know? Know – what happened to me?"

Now, I can say, "Yes, Dad, they know."

On days when I came home from Rosewood emotionally drained. On days when I felt unspeakable grief over the state of my loved ones. On days when I thought that I'd give anything if those who took care of them could have known them in their prime. On those days, it helped if I could talk with someone who understood. I hope this book helps you in such moments.

We who told our stories in *Minding Our Elders* were as honest as we could be, at the time of the telling. We weren't always proud of our thoughts. We weren't always proud of our actions. But we've hoped, in the telling, to heal a bit. To make some small sense of the pain. And, occasionally, to give a little comfort.

Thanks for listening. We're glad you were here.

To order additional copies of
MINDING OUR ELDERS
please complete the following.

$14.95 EACH
*(plus $3.95 shipping & handling for first book,
add $2.00 for each additional book ordered.*

*Shipping and Handling costs for larger quantites
available upon request.*

Please send me _____ additional books at $14.95 + shipping
& handling

Bill my: o VISA   o MasterCard   Expires _____

Card # _____

Signature _____

Daytime Phone Number _____

For credit card orders call 1-888-568-6329
TO ORDER ON-LINE VISIT: www.jmcompanies.com
OR SEND THIS ORDER FORM TO:
McCleery & Sons Publishing
PO Box 248
Gwinner, ND 58040-0248

I am enclosing $_____   o Check   o Money Order
Payable in US funds. No cash accepted.

SHIP TO:
Name_____

Mailing Address _____

City _____

State/Zip _____

Orders by check allow longer delivery time.
Money order and credit card orders will be shipped within 48 hours.
This offer is subject to change without notice.

McCLEERY & SONS
P U B L I S H I N G
a division of J&M Companies

Call 1-888-568-6329
to order by credit card OR order
on-line at www.jmcompanies.com

RECENT RELEASES

Great Stories of the Great Plains Vol. 2 - *Tales of the Dakotas*
There really is only one place in which you can relive the events of the great past that make up the history of North and South Dakota and that is in your mind. And that is our job, to set the stage for your imagination to take you on journeys into the history of this great region. With our books and radio show we try to bring to life, in your mind, the events that have made the Dakotas the great place they are to live in today. Written by Keith Norman - Author of *Great Stories of the Great Plains - Vol. 1* and *Great People of the Great Plains - Vol. 1* (144 pages)
$14.95 each in a 6x9" paperback.

It Really Happened Here & There
This takes off where Ethelyn Pearson's "It Really Happened Here!" left off... More entertaining stories and true accounts: The Mystery of the Headless Hermit, Herman Haunts Sauk Centre, Hunting Trip Gone Wrong, The Swinging of Thomas Brown, Moltan Hell Created Creeping Molasses Disaster, Preachers Do Too!, Skinned Alive, Run Into A Blizzard or Burn!, Life and Death of Ol' Mother Feather Legs, How the Dakotans Fought Off Rustlers, and much more!!!! Written by Ethelyn Pearson - Author of *It Really Happened Here!*
(136 pages) $24.95 each in an 8-1/2 x 11" paperback.

Great People of the Great Plains Vol. 1
25 Biographies of People Who Shaped the Dakotas
This is the second book for Keith Norman and the first in this series. Keith has always had an interest in the history of the region. His radio show 'Great Stories of the Great Plains' is heard on great radio stations all across both Dakotas. For more information on the radio show and a list of his current affiliates check out Norman's website at www.tumbleweednetwork.com. Written by Keith Norman (124 pgs.) $14.95 each in a 6x9" paperback.

History of Sargent County - Volume 2 - 1880-1920
(Forman, Gwinner, Milnor & Sargent County Veterans)
Over 220 photos and seven chapters containing: Forman, Gwinner and Milnor, North Dakota history with surveyed maps from 1909. Plus Early History of Sargent County, World War I Veterans, Civil War Veterans and Sargent County Fair History.
Written by: Susan Mary Kudelka - Author of *Early History of Sargent County - Volume 1* (224 pgs.)
$16.95 each in a 6x9" paperback.

History of Sargent County - Volume 3 - 1880-1920
(Brampton, Cayuga, Cogswell, Crete, DeLamere, Geneseo, Harlem, Havana, Rutland, Stirum & Other History)
Over 280 photos and fifteen chapters containing: Brampton, Cayuga, Cogswell, Crete, DeLamere, Geneseo, Harlem, Havana, Rutland and Stirum, North Dakota histories with surveyed maps from 1909. Plus history on Sargent County in WWI, Sargent County Newspapers, E. Hamilton Lee and bonus photo section.
Written by: Susan Mary Kudelka - Author of *Early History of Sargent County - Volume 1* (220 pgs.)
$16.95 each in a 6x9" paperback.

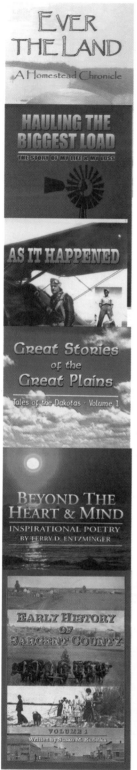

Ever The Land - *A Homestead Chronicle*

This historical chronicle (non-fiction) traces the life of young Pehr through his youth in the 1800's, marriage, parenthood and tenant farming in Sweden; then his emigration to America and homesteading in Minnesota. Multifarious simple joys and woes, and one deep constant sorrow accompany Pehr to his grave in 1914.
Written by: The late Ruben L. Parson (336 pgs.)
$16.96 each in a 6x9" paperback.

Hauling the Biggest Load - *The Story of My Life & My Loss*

This is an unusual story because of the many changes that have happened since the author's birth in 1926. In May 2002, he lost his son, John, in a car accident. None of those other experiences seemed important anymore... Richard needed something to try and take his mind off that tragedy. "I thought I had hauled some big loads in my life but I never had to have a load as big as this one."
Written by: Richard Hamann (144 pages)
$14.95 each in 6x9" paperback.

As It Happened

Over 40 photos and several chapters containing Allen Saunders' early years, tales of riding the rails, his Navy career, marriage, Army instruction, flying over "The Hump", and his return back to North Dakota. Written by Allen E. Saunders. (74 pgs)
$12.95 each in a 6x9" paperback.

Great Stories of the Great Plains - *Tales of the Dakotas - Vol. 1*

The radio show "Great Stories of the Great Plains" is heard on great radio stations all across both Dakotas. Norman has taken some of the stories from broadcasts, added some details, and even added some complete new tales to bring together this book of North and South Dakota history. Written by Keith Norman. (134 pgs.)
$14.95 each in a 6x9" paperback.

Beyond the Heart & Mind

Inspirational Poetry by Terry D. Entzminger

Beyond the Heart & Mind is the first in a series of inspirational poetry collections of Entzminger. Read and cherish over 100 original poems and true-to-the-heart verses printed in full color in the following sections: Words of Encouragement, On the Wings of Prayer, God Made You Very Special, Feelings From Within, The True Meaning of Love, and Daily Joys. (120 pgs.)
$12.95 each in a 6x9" paperback.

Early History of Sargent County - *Volume 1*

Over seventy photos and thirty-five chapters containing the early history of Sargent County, North Dakota: Glacial Movement in Sargent County, Native Americans in Sargent County, Weather, Memories of the Summer of 1883, Fight for the County Seat, Townships, Surveyed Maps from 1882 and much more.

Written by Susan M. Kudelka. (270 pgs.)
$16.95 each in a 6x9" paperback.

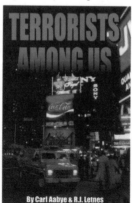

Terrorists Among Us

This piece of fiction was written to "expose a weakness" in present policies and conflicts in the masses of rules which seem to put emphasis on business, money, and power interests at the expense of the people's security, safety and happiness. Shouldn't we and our leaders strive for some security for our people? Written by Carl Aabye & R.J. Letnes. (178 pgs.)
$15.95 each in a 6x9" paperback.

THE HASTINGS SERIES

Blue Darkness *(First in a Series of Hastings Books)*
This tale of warm relationships and chilling murders takes place in the lake country of central Minnesota. Normal activities in the small town of New Dresen are disrupted when local resident, ex-CIA agent Maynard Cushing, is murdered. His killer, Robert Ranforth also an ex-CIA agent, had been living anonymously in the community for several years. Stalked and attached at his country home, Tom Hastings employs tools and people to mount a defense and help solve crimes. Written by Ernest Francis Schanilec (author of The Towers). (276 pgs.) $16.95 each in a 6x9" paperback.

The Towers *(Second in a Series of Hastings Books)*
Tom Hastings' move to Minneapolis was precipitated by the trauma associated with the murder of one of his neighbors. After renting a high-rise apartment in a building known as The Towers, he's met new friends and retained his relationship with a close friend, Julie, from St. Paul. Hastings is a resident for less than a year when a young lady is found murdered next to a railroad track, a couple of blocks from The Towers. The murderer shares the same elevators, lower-level garage and other areas in the high-rise as does Hastings. The building manager and other residents, along with Hastings are caught up in dramatic events that build to a crisis while the local police are baffled. Who is the killer? Written by Ernest Francis Schanilec. (268 pgs.) $16.95 each in a 6x9" paperback.

Danger In The Keys *(Third in a Series of Hastings Books)*
Tom Hastings is looking forward to a month's vacation in Florida. While driving through Tennessee, he witnesses an automobile leaving the road and plunging down a steep slope. The driver, a young woman, survives the accident. Tom is totally unaware that the young woman was being chased because she had chanced coming into possession of a valuable gem, which had been heisted from a Saudi Arabian prince. After arriving in Key Marie Island in Florida, Tom meets many interesting people, however, some of them are on the island because of the Guni gem, and they will stop at nothing in order to gain possession. Desperate people and their greedy ambitions interrupt Tom's goal of a peaceful vacation. Written by Ernest Francis Schanilec (210 pgs.) $16.95 each in a 6x9" paperback.

Purgatory Curve *(Fourth in a Series of Hastings Books)*
A loud horn penetrated the silence in New Dresden, Minnesota. Tom Hastings stepped onto the Main Street sidewalk and heard a freight train coming and watched in horror as it crushed a pickup truck that was stalled on the railroad tracks. Moments before the crash, he saw someone jump from the cab. An elderly farmer's body was later recovered from the mangled vehicle. Tom was interviewed by the sheriff the next day and was upset that his story about what he saw wasn't believed. The tragic death of the farmer was surrounded with controversy and mysterious people, including a nephew who taunted Tom after the accident. Or, was it an accident? Written by Ernest Francis Schanilec (210 pgs.) $16.95 each in a 6x9" paperback.

Gray Riders *(Fifth in a Series of Hastings Books)*
This is a flashback to Schanilec's Hastings Series mystery novels where Tom Hastings is the main character. Tom's great-grandfather, Thomas, lives on a farm with his family in western Missouri in 1861. The local citizenry react to the Union calvary by organizing and forming an armed group of horsemen who become known as the Gray Riders. The Riders not only defend their families and properties, but also ride with the Confederate Missouri Guard. They participate in three major battles. Written by Ernest Francis Schanilec. (266 pgs.) $16.95 each in a 6x9" paperback.

Sleep Six *(Fifth in a Series of Hastings Books)*
Revenge made Birdie Hec quit her job in Kansas City and move to New Dresden, Minnesota. A discovery after her mother's funeral had rekindled her memory of an abuse incident that had happened when she was six years old. An envelope containing six photographs, four of them with names, revealed some of her mother's abusers. Birdie moved into an apartment complex in New Dresden, using an anonymous name. She befriended three other women, who were all about the same age. While socializing with her new friends, Birdie scouted her potential victims. She plotted the demise of the four men whom she had definitely recognized...
Written by Ernest Francis Schanilec (250 pgs.) ISBN: 1-931916-40-3 $16.95 each in a 6x9" paperback.

NEW RELEASE

March on the Dakota's - *The Sibley Expedition of 1863*

Following the military action of 1862, the U. S. government began collecting an army at various posts and temporary stockades of the state, in preparation for a move northwestward to the Dakota Territories in the early summer of 1863. The campaign was organized by General John Pope, with the intent to subdue the Sioux. Two expeditions were planned, one under General H. H. Sibley, organized in Minnesota, and the other under the Command of General Alfred Sully. Interesting facts, actual accounts taken from soldiers' journals, campsite listings, casualties and record of troops also included. Written by Susan Mary Kudelka. (134pgs.)
$14.95 each in a 6x9" paperback.

War Child - *Growing Up in Adolf Hitler's Germany*

Annelee Woodstrom was 20 years old when she immigrated to America in 1947. These kind people in America wanted to hear about Adolf Hitler. During her adolescence, constant propaganda and strictly enforced censorship influenced her thinking. As a young adult, the bombings and all the consequential suffering caused by World War II affected Annelee deeply. How could Annelee tell them that as a child, during 1935, she wanted nothing more than to be a member of Adolf Hitler's Jung Maidens' organization? Written by Annelee Woodstrom (252 pgs.)
$16.95 each in a 6x9" paperback.

The SOE on Enemy Soil - *Churchill's Elite Force*

British Prime Minister Winston Churchill's plan for liberating Europe from the Nazis during the darkest days of the Second World War was ambitious: provide a few men and women, most of them barely out of their teens, with training in subversion and hand-to-hand combat, load them down with the latest in sophisticated explosives, drop them by parachute into the occupied countries, then sit back and wait for them to "Set Europe Ablaze." No story has been told with more honesty and humor than Sergeant Fallick tells his tale of service. The training, the fear, the tragic failures, the clandestine romances, and the soldiers' high jinks are all here, warmly told from the point of view of "one bloke" who experienced it all and lived to tell about it. Written by R.A. Fallick. (282 pgs.) $16.95 each in a 6x9" paperback.

Grandmother Alice

Memoirs from the Home Front Before Civil War into 1930's

Alice Crain Hawkins could be called the 'Grandma Moses of Literature'. Her stories, published for the first time, were written while an invalid during the last years of her life. These journal entries from the late 1920's and early 30's gives us a fresh, novel and unique understanding of the lives of those who lived in the upper part of South Carolina during the state's growing years. Alice and her ancestors experiences are filled with understanding - they are provacative and profound. Written by Reese Hawkins (178 pgs.) $16.95 each in a 6x9" paperback.

Tales & Memories of Western North Dakota *Prairie Tales & True Stories of 20th Century Rural Life*

This manuscript has been inspired with Steve's antidotes, bits of wisdom and jokes (sometimes ethnic, to reflect the melting pot that was and is North Dakota; and from most unknown sources). A story about how to live life with humor, courage and grace along with personal hardships, tragedies and triumphs. Written by Steve Taylor. (174 pgs.) $14.95 each in a 6x9" paperback.

Phil Lempert's HEALTHY, WEALTHY, & WISE
The Shoppers Guide for Today's Supermarket
This is the must-have tool for getting the most for your money in every aisle. With this valuable advice you will never see (or shop) the supermarket the same way again. You will learn how to: save at least $1,000 a year on your groceries, guarantee satisfaction on every shopping trip, get the most out of coupons or rebates, avoid marketing gimmicks, create the ultimate shopping list, read and understand the new food labels, choose the best supermarkets for you and your family. Written by Phil Lempert. (198 pgs.)
$9.95 each in a 6x9" paperback.

Miracles of COURAGE
The Larry W. Marsh Story
This story is for anyone looking for simple formulas for overcoming insurmountable obstacles. At age 18, Larry lost both legs in a traffic accident and learned to walk again on untested prosthesis. No obstacle was too big for him - putting himself through college - to teaching a group of children that frustrated the whole educational system - to developing a nationally recognized educational program to help these children succeed. Written by Linda Marsh. (134 pgs.)
$12.95 each in a 6x9" paperback.

The Garlic Cure
Learn about natural breakthroughs to outwit: Allergies, Arthritis, Cancer, Candida Albicans, Colds, Flu and Sore Throat, Environmental and Body Toxins, Fatigue, High Cholesterol, High Blood Pressure and Homocysteine and Sinus Headaches. The most comprehensive, factual and brightly written health book on garlic of all times. INCLUDES: 139 GOURMET GARLIC RECIPES! Written by James F. Scheer, Lynn Allison and Charlie Fox. (240 pgs.)
$14.95 each in a 6x9" paperback.

I Took The Easy Way Out
Life Lessons on Hidden Handicaps
Twenty-five years ago, Tom Day was managing a growing business - holding his own on the golf course and tennis court. He was living in the fast lane. For the past 25 years, Tom has spent his days in a wheelchair with a spinal cord injury. Attendants serve his every need. What happened to Tom? We get an honest account of the choices Tom made in his life. It's a courageous story of reckoning, redemption and peace. Written by Thomas J. Day. (200 pgs.)
$19.95 each in a 6x9" paperback.

9/11 and Meditation - *America's Handbook*
All Americans have been deeply affected by the terrorist events of and following 9-11-01 in our country. David Thorson submits that meditation is a potentially powerful intervention to ameliorate the frightening effects of such divisive and devastating acts of terror. This book features a lifetime of harrowing life events amidst intense pychological and social polarization, calamity and chaos; overcome in part by practicing the age-old art of meditation. Written by David Thorson. (110 pgs.)
$9.95 each in a 4-1/8 x 7-1/4" paperback.

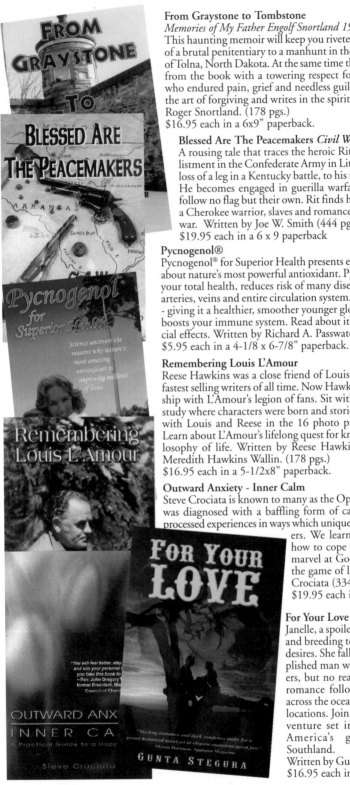

From Graystone to Tombstone
Memories of My Father Engolf Snortland 1908-1976
This haunting memoir will keep you riveted with true accounts of a brutal penitentiary to a manhunt in the unlikely little town of Tolna, North Dakota. At the same time the reader will emerge from the book with a towering respect for the author, a man who endured pain, grief and needless guilt -- but who learned the art of forgiving and writes in the spirit of hope. Written by Roger Snortland. (178 pgs.)
$16.95 each in a 6x9" paperback.

Blessed Are The Peacemakers *Civil War in the Ozarks*
A rousing tale that traces the heroic Rit Gatlin from his enlistment in the Confederate Army in Little Rock to his tragic loss of a leg in a Kentucky battle, to his return in the Ozarks. He becomes engaged in guerilla warfare with raiders who follow no flag but their own. Rit finds himself involved with a Cherokee warrior, slaves and romance in a land ravaged by war. Written by Joe W. Smith (444 pgs.)
$19.95 each in a 6 x 9 paperback

Pycnogenol®
Pycnogenol® for Superior Health presents exciting new evidence about nature's most powerful antioxidant. Pycnogenol® improves your total health, reduces risk of many diseases, safeguards your arteries, veins and entire circulation system. It protects your skin - giving it a healthier, smoother younger glow. Pycnogenol® also boosts your immune system. Read about it's many other beneficial effects. Written by Richard A. Passwater, Ph.D. (122 pgs.)
$5.95 each in a 4-1/8 x 6-7/8" paperback.

Remembering Louis L'Amour
Reese Hawkins was a close friend of Louis L'Amour, one of the fastest selling writers of all time. Now Hawkins shares this friendship with L'Amour's legion of fans. Sit with Reese in L'Amour's study where characters were born and stories came to life. Travel with Louis and Reese in the 16 photo pages in this memoir. Learn about L'Amour's lifelong quest for knowledge and his philosophy of life. Written by Reese Hawkins and his daughter Meredith Hawkins Wallin. (178 pgs.)
$16.95 each in a 5-1/2x8" paperback.

Outward Anxiety - Inner Calm
Steve Crociata is known to many as the Optician to the Stars. He was diagnosed with a baffling form of cancer. The author has processed experiences in ways which uniquely benefit today's readers. We learn valuable lessons on how to cope with distress, how to marvel at God, and how to win at the game of life. Written by Steve Crociata (334 pgs.)
$19.95 each in a 6 x 9 paperback

For Your Love
Janelle, a spoiled socialite, has beauty and breeding to attract any mate she desires. She falls for Jared, an accomplished man who has had many lovers, but no real love. Their hesitant romance follows Jared and Janelle across the ocean to exciting and wild locations. Join in a romance and adventure set in the mid-1800's in America's grand and proud Southland.
Written by Gunta Stegura. (358 pgs.)
$16.95 each in a 6x9" paperback.

Bonanza Belle

In 1908, Carrie Amundson left her home to become employed on a bonanza farm. Carrie married and moved to town. One tragedy after the other befell her and altered her life considerably and she found herself back on the farm where her family lived the toiled during the Great Depression. Carrie was witness to many life-changing events happenings. She changed from a carefree girl to a woman of great depth and stamina.
Written by Elaine Ulness Swenson. (344 pgs.)
$15.95 each in a 6x8-1/4" paperback.

Home Front

Read the continuing story of Carrie Amundson, whose life in North Dakota began in *Bonanza Belle*. This is the story of her family, faced with the challenges, sacrifices and hardships of World War II. Everything changed after the Pearl Harbor attack, and ordinary folk all across America, on the home front, pitched in to help in the war effort. Even years after the war's end, the effects of it are still evident in many of the men and women who were called to serve their country.
Written by Elaine Ulness Swenson. (304 pgs.)
$15.95 each in a 6x8-1/4" paperback.

First The Dream

This story spans ninety years of Anna's life - from Norway to America - to finding love and losing love. She and her family experience two world wars, flu epidemics, the Great Depression, droughts and other quirks of Mother Nature and the Vietnam War. A secret that Anna has kept is fully revealed at the end of her life. Written by Elaine Ulness Swenson. (326 pgs.)
$15.95 each in a 6x8-1/4" paperback

Pay Dirt

An absorbing story reveals how a man with the courage to follow his dream found both gold and unexpected adventure and adversity in Interior Alaska, while learning that human nature can be the most unpredictable of all.
Written by Otis Hahn & Alice Vollmar. (168 pgs.)
$15.95 each in a 6x9" paperback.

Spirits of Canyon Creek *Sequel to "Pay Dirt"*

Hahn has a rich stash of true stories about his gold mining experiences. This is a continued successful collaboration of battles on floodwaters, facing bears and the discovery of gold in the Yukon. Written by Otis Hahn & Alice Vollmar. (138 pgs.)
$15.95 each in a 6x9" paperback.

Seasons With Our Lord

Original seasonal and special event poems written from the heart. Feel the mood with the tranquil color photos facing each poem. A great coffee table book or gift idea. Written by Cheryl Lebahn Hegvik. (68 pgs.)
$24.95 each in a 11x8-1/2 paperback.

Damsel in a Dress

Escape into a world of reflection and after thought with this second printing of Larson's first poetry book. It is her intention to connect people with feelings and touch the souls of people who have experienced similiar times. Lynne emphasizes the belief that everything happens for a reason. After all, with every event in life come lessons...we grow from hardships. It gives us character and it made her who she is. Written by Lynne D. Richard Larson (author of <u>Eat, Drink & Remarry)</u> (86 pgs.)
$12.95 each in a 5x8" paperback.

Eat, Drink & Remarry

The poetry in this book is taken from different experiences in Lynne's life and from different geographical and different emotional places. Every poem is an inspiration from someone or a direct event from their life...or from hers. Every victory and every mistake - young or old. They slowly shape and mold you into the unique person you are. Celebrate them as rough times that you were strong enough to endure. Written by Lynne D. Richard Larson (86 pgs.) $12.95 each in a 5x8" paperback.

Country-fied

Stories with a sense of humor and love for country and small town people who, like the author, grew up country-fied . . . Country-fied people grow up with a unique awareness of their dependence on the land. They live their lives with dignity, hard work, determination and the ability to laugh at themselves.
Written by Elaine Babcock. (184 pgs.)
$14.95 each in a 6x9" paperback.

Charlie's Gold and Other Frontier Tales

Kamron's first collection of short stories gives you adventure tales about men and women of the west, made up of cowboys, Indians, and settlers. Written by Kent Kamron.
(174 pgs.) $15.95 each in a 6x9" paperback.

A Time For Justice

This second collection of Kamron's short stories takes off where the first volume left off, satisfying the reader's hunger for more tales of the wide prairie. Written by Kent Kamron. (182 pgs.) $16.95 each in a 6x9" paperback.

It Really Happened Here!

Relive the days of farm-to-farm salesmen and hucksters, of ghost ships and locust plagues when you read Ethelyn Pearson's collection of strange but true tales. It captures the spirit of our ancestors in short, easy to read, colorful accounts that will have you yearning for more. Written by Ethelyn Pearson. (168 pgs.) $24.95 each in an 8-1/2x11" paperback.

The Silk Robe - Dedicated to Shari Lynn Hunt, a wonderful woman who passed away from cancer. Mom lived her life with unfailing faith, an open loving heart and a giving spirit. She is remembered for her compassion and gentle strength. Written by Shaunna Privratsky.
$6.95 each in a 4-1/4x5-1/2" booklet. *Complimentary notecard and envelope included.*

(Add $3.95 shipping & handling for first book, add $2.00 for each additional book ordered.)